Positive

Thinking

*Reap the Advantage of Unshakeable Mindset and
Remove Negativity and Stress Using Secret
Psychology, Gratitude, Discipline and Powerful
Imaging Techniques*

Becca Earl

Chapter 1: How To Handle The Bad Stuff.......................... 1

Chapter 2: Ways To A Stress-Free Life 8

Chapter 3: Roadblocks To Positive Mindset..................... 16

Chapter 4: Benefits Of Positive Thinking 20

Chapter 5: Benefits Of Positive Thinking On One's Social
Life 26

Chapter 6: How Negativity Can Be A Dream Killer 31

Chapter 7: Benefits Of Positive Thinking 42

Chapter 8: What Worry Does To You?.............................. 47

Chapter 9: Knowing What You Want In Life...................... 52

Chapter 10: The Power Of Belief 59

Chapter 11: Positive Energy Techniques........................... 65

Chapter 12: Practice Gratitude 69

Chapter 13: Start At One 77

Chapter 14: Replacing Negative With Positive................. 80

Chapter 15: The Pessimist 90

Chapter 16: Don't Sweat The Small Stuff......................... 93

Chapter 17: Exercises To Control Your Thoughts 97

Chapter 18: Imagination: Our Creative Ability............... 105

Chapter 19: The Secret 111

Chapter 20: Don't Run Away From Fear 117

Chapter 21: Positive Thinking And Your Career 122

Chapter 22: Positive Thinking And Health 130

Chapter 23: How To Change The Odds Of A Happy Life . 145

Chapter 24: Conduct A Self-Inventory 149

Chapter 25: Making It Part Of Your Life 152

Chapter 26: How To Create A Happy You 159

Chapter 27: The New You 171

Chapter 28: How To Adopt This Attitude Now 174

Chapter 29: Eliminating Negative Triggers 182

Chapter 30: Putting Positive Thinking Into Practice 196

Chapter 31: Can You "Force" Yourself Into Happiness? . 206

Chapter 32: How To Solve Personal Problems 215

Chapter 33: Ways To Overcome Negative Thinking For Good 218

Chapter 34: Improve Your Self-Talk By Conquering Your Mind 225

Chapter 35: The Self-Assured Mindset 230

Chapter 36: Applying Positive Thinking To Larger Life Goals 233

Chapter 37: Training The Mind To Have Positive Thoughts Always 237

Chapter 38: The Word And Thought Game 242

Chapter 39: They Are All Mine, And Hence I Cannot Let Go 248

Chapter 1: How To Handle The Bad Stuff.

Think it through

Life can throw some real curve balls. You may be having fun baking cookies with your kids, the phone rings and you find out your husband has been taken to the hospital. How do you stay positive in such a situation? The first thing to do is to examine what just happened.

Here is the situation. You have to get out of cooking and baking mode, figure out what to do with the kids and get to the hospital. Except, your car is in the garage. You could easily stand there screaming and telling yourself, "I can't handle this," or you can take one positive step at a time. Figure out the primary problem. In this case, it seems to be lack of a car; call a friend or a cab. Problem two is what to do with the kids; throw some shoes on them and take them with you, or ask a friend to watch them. Problem three is the cookies; they are not a problem, turn off the oven and leave the mess. Following the steps of one positive action after another, you are now on the way to the hospital. You have not wasted precious time and energy worrying about how bad the situation is and throwing your hands in the air.

Become self-sufficient

One way to boost your confidence and positively address the normal obstacles and events in your life is to become self-sufficient. Becoming self-reliant reduces your dependence on other people and can actually save you money. You may be surprised at some of the things people think they cannot do, or panic over it if they are faced with having to do them.

Here is an example that I read about. Are you a driver who does not know how to change a tire? If you get a flat, do you have to rely on roadside assistance to help you out?

There is nothing wrong with having roadside assistance, but why would a person want to stand around, often on a deserted road in the middle of nowhere, and wait for a person driving a tow truck to come change a tire? In my area, it takes 45 minutes for the truck to come, at the very least. It is my choice to change the tire myself and get back on the road, instead of waiting around for an undisclosed amount of time. This is just one simple task that, if learned, can change your day from having to deal with an inconvenience to one of a chain of inconveniences.

Let's take a look at cooking. Perhaps you do not know how to cook, and eat most of your meals out and put the rest in the microwave. You have two problems here; the first is that you are not eating healthy, and the second is that you are wasting money. Go out and buy yourself a cookbook written for children. Once you learn the basics and start experimenting and cooking, you can eliminate up to 75% or more of your food costs by not eating out. If you have children, teach them how to cook as soon as they show an interest in it. Even a small child can tear the salad lettuce. When a family cooks together, they build positive bonds through conversation and sharing. While you are at it, cook extra so you can freeze it for when you are in a hurry. When you cook your own food and eat healthier, you will feel better. Feeling good makes you happier.

There are many things you can learn, such as simple electrical wiring, plumbing and other home maintenance. Of course there are instances where you will have to call in a professional, but most people can learn how to change a light switch, stop a leaking toilet flapper or use a drain snake. Also, make sure you know how to shut off the electricity, water and gas to your house. This can also save you money.

When you reduce your dependence on other people you will not only save money, you will feel the good feeling of a sense of accomplishment. Learn what you can and keep learning. Remember to call in the professionals when something is above your skill level, however; it is not necessary to be proficient at everything, but it is good to learn enough to do the simple tasks.

Being self-sufficient raises your confidence level, provides a sense of accomplishment when the skills are used, and enables you to be more positive about your ability to handle the events which come your way.

Act it out.

If you do not know how to act positive, take a look around you and observe others who are. These people may be co-workers, friends, family or celebrities of any age or from any time. Just make sure they have the quality you are looking for. Find out what a happy person looks like, and then look happy.

Smile, smile a lot, even if you have to force yourself. Smile for one full minute and see how much better you feel. A smile a day keeps the doctor away. Researchers have discovered a connection between a positive attitude and good health. The bigger the smile, the more frequent the smile, the more apt a person is to be positive and healthy.

Smiling is a choice; even when life is throwing a curve ball or two your way, can still smile if you choose. All you have to do is pull the lips back and grin.

If you say you have nothing to smile about, you are incorrect. Look at the beauty all around you. If you can see, you have something to smile about. Think about those who can't see and then you might be able to smile.

Smiling is simple and easy to master if you have the desire to change your life. You can have a positive effect on others today just by practicing your smile. Give everyone you meet today a smile and see what happens.

Chapter 2: Ways To A Stress-Free Life

"Adopting the right attitude can convert a negative stress into a positive one."

-Hans Selye

Many people don't see the good side of things because they are too preoccupied dealing with their worries, fears, anxieties and stressors. Stress has always been perceived as something negative but it is so ironic that people always seem to look for things to stress about. When they wake up in the morning, they think of what they are going to wear, how they are going to reach their office in the fastest possible way, whom they are going to have lunch with and what time they could get back home. These simple things may seem so uncomplicated and benign, but the truth is, they can cause great worries and unnecessary stress at the end of the day.

No matter what you do, and no matter how you try to avoid it, stress will always be there, waiting around the corner for you to come and get it. In fact, you need it to function properly. For example, you are preparing for an exam or work presentation tomorrow and you are feeling some stress about it. To relieve some of the stress, what you do is you study and prepare for it. Though stress here is something that you don't see as positive, your response to it is. The next thing you know is that you did very well of the exam or presentation! Imagine if you are not worried about your exam. The most likely thing you'd do is you won't prepare for it. Sometimes, not feeling the stress is more dangerous because you don't perceive any harm and your body as a harmless situation.

Stress takes on different forms. It can be mild, which is something that you can easily overcome, or it could be something more severe, something that can exhaust you of your energy and resources. Mild stress, just like the example given above, is helpful because it keeps you prepared for what's going to happen. But if the stress is so severe that you don't know what to do anymore, then it becomes harmful.

When you feel that you can no longer perform well in your job, or when you can no longer think straight, or when you think that you are not anymore getting the results that you want to achieve, you are likely undergoing severe stress. At this point, it is not advisable to continue with what you are doing. Just like a machine that has been excessively used, people inefficiently function when they are under severe stress. Eliminating the stressors is not easy but there are ways you can do it.

Don't try to control everything

People have the tendency to control everything: their time, money, and other people. What they don't know is that they get most of the stress comes from trying to control everything. It's not bad to be carefree every once in a while. Give yourself some freedom by not thinking about your bills at home, your work deadlines and the traffic jam outside. Recognize that at the moment these things are out of your control.

You can avoid thinking about them. Change your mindset. You can use the analogy of a dresser. In the bottom drawer you can store all your stresses and worries. In the top drawer you can store all your happy thoughts and things you're grateful for. So if you're having difficulty changing your mindset or thoughts, go ahead and place them in the bottom drawer and grab something from the top one.

Spend one hour a day without technology

It is true that technology plays an important role in people's lives. However, it is also true that it takes up a large part of one's time. People are meant for interaction and socialization. Though technology, like smartphones, tablets and computers are meant for communication, people nowadays forget and do not seem to bother talking with their classmates, co-workers and neighbors. It is as if their minds have been taken over by these gadgets.

These gadgets can be a source of additional stress. Spending one hour a day (or longer) without them would be a helpful way of relieving your stress. It can be very challenging for some to not check their email or look at their phone for even one hour. Instead of interacting with your smart phone or computer, talk with the people around you, laugh out loud with them and share stories with them. You'll see how refreshing and energizing this can be.

For more information on strategies for telling stories, and strategies for talking to strangers and making new friends, check out: The Storytelling Method, and The Conversation Method, which will give your social life a new set of wings.

Take a Time Out

Time out is for those who are brave enough to take a step back and rethink of everything. Taking a time out does not mean giving up; it just means that there are some things that you need to take care of before proceeding to the next step. In a sense, it's a way to unwind and look at the big picture and refocus on what is important about whatever you are currently working on.

Stress often results from too much work and not giving your body or mind enough time to relax. Give yourself a break from working. Taking short work breaks each hour increases productivity. Even a short 2 – 5 minute break to stretch your body, or 5 minutes to walk around or 5 minutes to step outside and get some fresh air will help. When you continue working despite exhaustion, you may produce unsatisfactory results that can further aggravate your stress. Some people like to meditate and others like to take a walk to clear their mind. So go ahead and take that time-out.

Live in the present moment

Most of the anxiety, worry, and stress that you feel arise from thinking about the future or the past. You stress about 'what if's'. What if you did this or what if you did not do that? You worry whether it's going to rain or whether you can meet the deadline of your assignment. Live in the present so that much of your worries and anxiety will be eliminated. A rule I like to use is the 80/20 rule – spending 80% of my time enjoying the present moment, and 20% of my time thinking of the future or what I can learn from my past. Life is most fun and relaxing when you are enjoying the present moment.

If you want to learn more about how to live in the present moment, I highly recommend my book titled How To Live In the Present Moment, which has proven to be an eye-opening experience for many readers.

Chapter 3: Roadblocks To Positive Mindset

The process of developing a positive mindset is a bit challenging, especially if you are already used to thinking toxic and extremely negative thoughts, but rest assured that with practice, you can make it a part of your life. The first step is to identify the roadblocks that could be stopping you from cultivating a more positive attitude. Once you identified them, it will be easier for you to make positivity a natural part of your system.

Your tendency to bully yourself

If you want to develop a more positive mindset, then it's time to be kind to yourself. Avoid setting standards that you will have a hard time meeting. While it's okay for you to dream of doing well all the time, expecting to become better than the best then blaming yourself in case you fail is an act of bullying yourself. Stop blaming and bullying yourself. Try living in the present and moving forward with a more positive attitude in case of failures.

Your own beliefs

Your own beliefs may also stop you from cultivating a more positive mindset. Recognize the fact that you have full control of your thoughts and beliefs. While it's impossible for you to control the things that are happening outside, you can actually control how you react to certain situations. You have the power to influence your inner world – your thoughts and beliefs. It is crucial to maximize such power if you want to develop positivity.

Internal conflict

This roadblock has the tendency to sabotage all your efforts to cultivating a positive mindset without you even knowing it. Internal conflict makes you more prone to experience disharmony in your inner beings. This is the main reason why you need to discover your deepest personal values and standards. To avoid internal conflict, and create harmony instead, live and act based on your core values. You have to pay close attention to this roadblock, especially if you have the tendency to sabotage yourself.

Resistance to change

Another roadblock that may stop you from developing a positive mindset is your resistance to change. To deal with this problem, practice letting go. Be willing to let go of the beliefs, thoughts, struggles and other things that prevent you from enjoying life. Break your emotional attachments to negative things and thoughts. Be willing to change for the better, instead of hanging on to your old self. Let go of anything that does not do good on you.

The road to achieving a positive mindset is long, and a bit challenging, but with focus and determination, you can successfully develop it. You will most likely face the roadblocks mentioned above, but rest assured that it is easy to beat them, provided you put your heart and mind to embracing positivity.

The next chapters of this book will provide you with daily tasks within a 21-day period. Doing the tasks every day can help increase your chances of successfully cultivating a mind filled with only positive and happy thoughts.

Chapter 4: Benefits Of Positive Thinking

Positive thinking brings a lot of good things in the lives of people that practice it. You have more than one reason to stay positive in life. These are the reasons that should motivate one to strive to think positively at all times.

Positive thinking brings happiness

A positive attitude will be the one to awaken your happiness. Many people associate happiness with riches but what they do not know is that happens is derived from one's attitude. This is because happiness comes from deep within you and not from what is on the outside. When you are always thinking of how good things are and how good they ought to be, you can be sure that you will be a happy person. On the other hand negative thoughts will always make you sulky and unhappy.

Positive thinking betters one's health

Good health is what is required by every person for people to enjoy a longer life. Positive thinking brings more energy and good health to people. Now that you see many possibilities in life, you become more energized to try out as many as you can, if not all of them. Positive people are also happier and this helps reduce stress and anxiety, which affects the health of many people in this life. That is why health experts are always sure that one's health can get better if they change the way that they think and feel. Our thinking has great effects on your body and general health. When you think positively, you will be able to deal with some of the things that affect your health and your immune systems gets better. You can even get better faster if you are already feeling sick.

Positive thinking motivates you

If you have set goals and you really want to achieve them, you just have to think positively and achieving those goals will be a lot easier. Positive thoughts helps a person to accomplish their dreams and achieve their goals and it helps a person handle all tasks he faces in life. Everyone needs motivation because it is the force that pushes one forward and encourages one to go for what he needs to get what he wants in life. You are able to overcome obstacles along the way with motivation, therefore stay positive and achieve so much in life.

Positive thinking boosts one's self esteem

The way you think and the attitude that you have towards yourself has everything to do with the way you feel about yourself. Self-esteem is very important because it determines how you feel from deep within. It is impossible to love other people if you do not love yourself, therefore everything starts with the way that you feel about yourself. If therefore you have a positive mind you can always think of good things about yourself and this will change the way that you think and feel about other people. To achieve this, start seeing good things in you, things that make you a better person. See how much you can do and not what you are not able to do. People will not manage to bring you down if you think highly about yourself. If you respect yourself, people will automatically show respect for you.

Start by loving yourself, and being kind to yourself. Harbor positive expressions at all times and you will bring out self-confidence and an inner strength that you never thought you had in the beginning.

Positivity betters your relationships

A positive person will always see good things in other people and this is one way to promotes better relationships. When you start thinking positively about yourself, you will start appreciating other people and their flaws, since you start realizing that you are all the same.

Positive thinking makes a person more likeable. People are always attracted to people who are happier and positive in life. If you do not like working in a team, or going out for some fun, people will start avoiding you but if you show that you are always up to something good and exciting, you will have people come closer to you. It is easy to make friends and to keep friends when you are positive than when you are negative. When you are happy, you can always work better with other people than when you are stressed up and sad.

Positivity builds your skill set

Positive thoughts will help you build and strengthen your skills that you will always use in life. Positive emotions will help you build sets of skills that will make it possible for you to deal with other kinds of emotions that you face in life. A happy person will always socialize better with other people and this helps to build social skills that will be significant for the rest of their lives. An outgoing personality begins to form from the time when a person is very young. If the personality is maintained, it can bring out a set of creative skills and social skills that will make you a better person in life.

Chapter 5: Benefits Of Positive Thinking On One's Social Life

The benefits of being a positive thinker go outside of one's physical and psychological aspects. Do you know that having more lasting and fulfilling relationships are also part of the benefits of being a positive thinker? Indeed. Again, studies have revealed that those who are optimistic have the tendency to have deeper and more rewarding friendships, husband and wife relationship and family connections. How? The simple truth is this – positive thinkers are happier people. When one is happy, there is increased capacity to look outside the self and focus on other things and people. Therefore, the positive thinkers have increased capacity to love, share joys, and extend hospitality and warmth to others.

Positive thinkers are also noted to be kinder and more considerate to other people. This is why they have more number of friends as they are more liked by other people. The surveys also revealed that they are easier to get along with and more fun to be with. Another good thing about these positive thinkers is their ability to identify the things they need to change about themselves. Then they do these things that would help make them better partners or friends to others. They do not blame other people and force them to change their ways.They focus on improving themselves, instead.

Aside from these characteristics, the positive thinkers are better at handling any given relationship because of the following reasons:

1. They are better communicators. Communication is one very important aspect of any relationship. In the event that there is a misunderstanding, these people are more likely to initiate a discussion and settle the disagreement. They also tend to focus on the solution

and not linger on the problem itself. Positive thinkers are more open and better listeners, too. They give time for other people to verbalize their concerns. Plus, another good quality is they know when to accept if they are wrong and apologize for it.

2.   They are friendlier. Maybe because they feel good about themselves or they just like to be with other people. Positive thinkers are more likely to initiate introductions, smile and become friends with others. As they are more outgoing and extrovert, they aremore involved in activities dealing with other people. Thus, they are better at keeping friends and increasing their acquaintances.

3.   They are more fun to be with. Honestly, whom would you rather be with? Someone who is gloomy and expects the worst or one who is happy and has a positive outlook in life? Depressed people can be tiresome to accompany while happy and energetic people keep you up

and happy, too. Positive thinkers usually possess great sense of humor. They can also laugh at their own mistakes.

4. They are flexible. When nothing turns according to schedule, the positive thinkers do not flinch and get irritated at the changes. They usually easily adapt to changes and thrive. They are open to new things. They are not afraid to get out of their comfort zones and rock their boats. In an organization, you would know the positive thinkers on how they would welcome whatever changes are required. You would seldom see them grumble and complain. Instead, you would already see them actively participating in the planning of the changes.

5. They focus on the good rather than the bad in their partners, friends and coworkers. Positive thinkers enjoy great and harmonious relationships because they tend to put their attention on the good qualities and performances of other peoplerather than dwell on their negative

characteristics and mistakes. They are also more appreciative and vocal about it, too.

6.   They tend not to harbor ill feelings towards other people. They are forgiving and they usually do not amplify errors, especially those that were unintentional. They always see the good in the other person.

When a person has a positive disposition in life, other people gravitate towards him or her. There is an attraction and a desire to be with that person. If you want to have more friends, a happier family life and more satisfying relationships with other people, learn to become more positive in your thoughts, in your words and in your actions. Your social life would certainly benefit greatly just by being more positive in life.

Chapter 6: How Negativity Can Be A Dream Killer

Negativity is the main reason why so many dreamers' dreams diminish. Where do all the dreamers' dreams go? Take the kid who dreamt of being a rock star but grew up to work in finance. How about the teacher who wanted to become a lawyer but due to the negative influencers in her life, took an easier route? Or how about the salesperson who wanted to be cast as Juliet in a featured Broadway show; singing, dancing, and giving her best performance on the Broadway stage each night?

I had a friend by the name of D.O. tell me the other day that she wanted to be a best-selling author of comic books. As a young child she would always get into trouble because she would draw on almost everything in her house;

sometimes even on the furniture. She loved the idea of creating characters from scratch and making them come alive. She dreamt of having a series of her comic book collections published in the New York Times. She even dreamt of her characters becoming cartoon characters on Disney. When I asked her why she didn't pursue her dreams of becoming the big comic book writer, she said that, at the time, she had other influencers around her who thought it was a foolish dream to follow; she still regrets to this day not giving it a try. She ended up making a choice between working in the dental field, rather than chasing a dream that would have given her the utmost satisfaction.

It's amazing how negative thoughts can deteriorate the one thing we once treasured as children: our dreams. Any time a person places negative ideas or thoughts in our heads, we start doubting our own objectives. When negativity is freely roaming in our brains at full capacity, that's when the real tug of war with positivity starts.

On the other hand, I have a friend who did, in fact, follow her dreams of becoming a designer. She took all of those negative thoughts and ideas and used them to jump-start her career. Today she travels around the world designing garments for well-known individuals. She had a dream that cost her many sleepless nights and that dream was bigger than Jupiter and Mars both combined. Sure, she had a few set-backs along the way, but she never allowed those negative influencers to steal her future goals and desires.

Having positive thoughts about yourself, your dreams, and your desires are the vehicle towards a successful future.

Negativity Toxicity

I'm probably one of the most negative people on the planet, or at least I used to be. I used to wear negativity like it was the hottest trending fashion. Me and Negativity were so popular that we always sat in VIP; we were best friends. However, that same friend blocked me from many opportunities and kept me captive for years. Negativity had controlled my world and I was his puppet.

Even as a young child negativity would show up from time to time. I remember when I was twelve I went to one of my friend's house for a sleepover. This particular friend of mine went to the best schools and lived in the best neighborhood. I remember her mother at one point asking me to do a math equation and then asked her daughter to do that same equation. I was no dummy; I knew that she was trying to compare me to her daughter. I did realize at that very moment that I was being judged. As a young preteen that moment crushed my spirit. Sadly, I was being judged for my parents' inability to send me to the best school.

In addition, if you were to factor-in my environment, let's just say that I did not grow up in Beverly Hills and my zip code was definitely no 90210. Not always, but sometimes, when your environment is not the most ideal, people immediately judge you.

In addition, sometimes even as adults, we say negative things to children that can leave a long-term negative emotional scar. We also say negative things to children which forces them to prove the world wrong. Ever met someone who was told at a young age that they would never amount to anything? And then that person grows up to be the greatest inspiration of all time? Life is full of many endless possibilities and when you learn how to redirect the negative and increase the positive thoughts, your results will improve.

Holding Hands With Fear

Fear and negativity are a match made in heaven. Fear cannot fester without negative thoughts. When fear is present, negative thoughts appear and then doubt immediately kicks in. Fear is the ultimate monster that hides under our beds, in our closets and in our minds. Fear is the doorkeeper that can sometimes lock-out every dream, opportunity, or goal that one is seeking to achieve. As children, some of us feared the boogie monster; as adults, some of us fear making life-changing choices.

I knew a woman by the name of V.T. who always made-up excuses as to why she never went to college; one minute it was because of money, the next minute it was because her family did not support her career decisions of her wanting to pursue her dreams of becoming a nurse. They believed that although nursing was a great field, it was a downgrade from being a doctor. "Why be a nurse when you can just study a few more years and become a doctor?"

Although the woman appreciated her parent's feedback, their negativity also increased her doubt. One day, we were having lunch and she finally told me why she didn't go to college. It had nothing to do with money, nor her family pressuring her to go to school to become a doctor. She didn't want to go to college because she didn't think that she was smart enough to take on such a challenge. In her mental state, becoming a nurse or doctor would be an ideal career. However, because she allowed fear to consume her career path, she ended settling and working multiple jobs instead.

A quote from the Da Vinci Code by Dan Brown states that, "Men go to far greater lengths to avoid what they fear than to obtain what they desire." Sometimes when a person allows fear to control every decision being made, they can become paralyzed towards the idea of moving forward. In addition, negative thoughts begin to pour in and flood out positive growth.

I met a woman a few months ago who had been at her company for over fourteen years. This was the first job that she had after being a stay at home mom for years. She had recently gone through a divorce and only had two years to go before she could retire. Her job started downsizing and making cuts and she ended up getting laid off. She ended up losing everything including her pension, and this devastated her; her once promising retirement was now gone. Her biggest fear had now become her reality, and she was now standing in the unemployment line. Part of her fear was that she was in her late 60s and she didn't believe that anyone would hire her due to her age. When a person conditions their brain into believing that they are never going to succeed, they ultimately set themselves up for failure.

Here are some of the most common thoughts and ideas we tell ourselves:

"I'm never going to get the job because I'm too old or young."

"I'm not pretty enough."

"I'm never going to be able to pay off my debt."

"I'm not capable of handling such a challenging task."

"I'm never going to win this big account that I've been working on over the course of weeks."

"I'm never going to get promoted because I lack certain knowledge or skills."

"I'm never going to get into a good school."

"I don't have time to study; I have to work late."

"I'm never going to invest my money into the stock market because I'm going to lose my money."

"I'm not smart enough."

"I'm never going to buy a house because of upkeeps."

"I'm never going to get the job because of my lack of experience."

All of these negative thoughts are driven out of fear. We say these negative things because we fear the outcome. Fearing the outcomes for some people is even scarier than the results. In most cases, one would rather avoid taking chances vs. taking action.

When we allow fear to overpower our thoughts, we allow negative ideas to win-over our emotions. S.R. Crawford states that, "There is a lot of negativity and bad habits that just need to be cut out of our lives. Sometimes we hold on tightly to the things that are actually causing us a lot of pain. We are our own worst enemy. We cling to all the wrong things. We subconsciously do things that are very bad for us, the worst being that we tell ourselves every day that "we're not good enough" and "it's our fault. Well cut it out!" Before you can mentally kick negativity in the face, first you have to grab hold of your fears, lock them down, and then come-up with an action plan.

Chapter 7: Benefits Of Positive Thinking

A positive attitude and way of thinking can improve your overall well-being while helping you cope with the daily aspects of life more easily. Research today shows that positive thinking is much more than just being joyful and cheerful or displaying an bubbly attitude. Positive thoughts can actually create real significance in your life and help you build skills that last much longer than you can think.

Below are eight benefits derived from positive thinking.

Optimism

Positive thinking gives you more energy and more joy. You will see that as you cultivate positivity in your mind and in your heart, you will find it easier achieve greater power and inner strength. The success and self-confidence creates an overall sense of optimism allowing you to achieve greater feats.

Improves Resilience

Being resilient is the unique capability to cope with any form difficulty that you may encounter. A positive thinker will courageously face the situation and will not be afraid to encounter stress and suffering. With a healthy mind and body, optimism helps a person to bounce back from any kind of hardshisps after dealing with the challenge.

Happiness and Success

Positive thinking has the power to change the environment around you and your whole life. Positive attitude helps you attract other like-minded people like yourself therefore changing the people and environment around you. Positive thinking develops the ability to not only motivate yourself but also to inspire and motivate others to be successful and happy.

Improved Focus

Positive thinking helps you deliberate on finding a solution instead of focusing on the undesirable elements and losing valuable time. It enhances your constructive and creative thinking is. While a people with a negative attitude or mindset are so distracted that they may not even seek a solution.

Busting Stress

When a positive thinker is confronted with a stressful situation he handles it better for the same reason as mentioned above, improved focus. When feel less stress, when you worry less. The power of positive thinking lowers overall stress levels and increases your life span.

Improved Health

Your thought have a direct influence on your body and its functions. Positive thinkers not only tend to have lower risks of disease but also have a better psychological and physical well-being.

Self Esteem

When you embrace an optimistic outlook you tend to have confidence in yourself and your abilities. You begin to have faith in your potential which gives you the motivation to set as well as achieve your goals.

More problem solving skills

A person with a positive attitude is always optimistic and says 'Yes I can'. The positive energy helps to keep the mind calm and solve problems with improved analytical capabilities.

Chapter 8: What Worry Does To You?

While there's the general illusion amongst most people that worrying enough can prevent certain bad things from occurring, this in not practically the case! Worrying can harm your body and mind in ways you have never imagined. For instance, when normal worrying becomes pathological, excessive worrying — feelings of high anxiety result, which in turn might negatively impact your general well-being.

Scientists have established that worrying has a 'minus' effect on your health. To start with, ageing faster, getting more stressed, tired and depressed are just a few of the negative implications.

The science behind this is fairly simple.

When you get excessively worried, your body reacts to the anxiety generated in the same way it would respond to physical danger. Your brain has to prepare your body for the intense physical demands that it's just about to ask of it. Basically, the brain does this by stimulating the release of adrenalin and stress hormone cortisol into your bloodstream. As a result, the heart beats faster, breathing gets heavier and you are also likely to profusely sweat.

The 'fight or flight' status takes hold of your entire body.

But then, the 'dangers' that make us worry cannot be addressed by a 'fight or flight' response. So your body remains alert. The stress hormone cortisol and adrenalin are still in the bloodstream. When this happens for extended periods of time, increased toxicity in the body affects your heart, nervous system as well as the glands, leading to a plethora of unpleasant illnesses – including but not limited to stomach ulcers and heart attacks. The excessive stress hormones within the bloodstream are known to cause a number of physical reactions:

• Irritability

- Fatigue
- Dry mouth
- Dizziness
- Nervous energy
- Rapid breathing

- Breath shortness
- Sweating
- Trembling and twitching
- Digestive disorders
- Short-term loss of memory
- Early coronary artery disease

The extra 'alertness' and tensing also leads to muscle aches, headaches and back pains. Worse still, the immune system takes more time to respond to common infections. RED ALERT!

Effects on your Mind

Peace of mind becomes a thing of the past. It's harder to concentrate and remember things. More so, it might be next-to-impossible to find sleep at night. Libido-loss has also been understood to be a common effect of excessive worrying. Having a fulfilling sex life has everything to do with feeling healthy and relaxed both in the body and mind. When you're worn down by worry, the fulfilling sex life becomes elusive.

When crippled by worry, absent-mindedness sets in. It gets harder to pay attention to your health. As a result, you might feel too stressed to eat. This effectively deprives your body of the necessary minerals and nutrients, creating a score board for rapid ageing and poor health.

See what worry does to you?

By dispelling away all the worrying thoughts, you can dramatically enhance the quality of your life as well as put multiple health and mental problems at bay. In the next chapter, we look at how you can get rid of worry, whatever its sources or causes.

Chapter 9: Knowing What You Want

In Life

The whole idea behind knowing what you want in life is so that you can find meaning and purpose. It is a chance to create awareness of who you are as a person and what you set out to achieve. If you find yourself living in circles and by that I mean working hard, but you never seem to get anywhere worthwhile, then it means you didn't take some time to determine what you want in life.

For anyone to achieve satisfaction in life, they have to focus on things that they believe complete them. You are only aware of these things if you determine the exact thing you want in life and the path you would like to follow to achieve them. This should be applicable in all areas of your life. It is impossible to work towards achieving something when you have no idea what it is you want to achieve. Finding direction is important and will make it easier for you to make your dreams a reality.

It is a challenge for many to determine what they want in life, but if you are really ambitious about making a difference then you need to work at it. Below are important ways that I believe will help you know what you want in life:

1) Family and friends: These are the people whom you spend a big part of your life with and could help you know what you want in life. They will advise on the things that they know you always enjoy and what they believe would be best for you depending on how well they know you.

2) Knowledge and skills: There are always those specific things that you are excellent at and are equipped with the required knowledge and skills to progress in life through them. This could be something you studied in school or is a talent you grew with. Going back to yourself, analyzing and searching, will help you

know who you really want to be in life. This will be the beginning of a great life.

3) Goal setting: Another great way of knowing what you want in life is through setting goals. Have your short term and long term goals written down and they are the ones that will give you a clear idea of what you want in life. Goals have, for a long time, been known to be a source of motivation and direction and are exactly what you need.

4) Know where your happiness: As I said the most important thing everyone should be in search of is happiness. If you are aware of certain things that always make you happy, then you already have an answer to the question at hand. Take some time to reach deep into yourself and know the kind of things that always make you happy.

AFFIRMATIONS FOR GROWTH AND DEVELOPMENT

Affirmations are short sentences that are always believed to have a huge effect on a person's life. They normally affect the conscious and subconscious mind and their words bring up mental images that have the ability to motivate, inspire and energize. If you make it a habit of always repeating specific affirmations, then the resultant images brought about will influence a person's habits, behaviors, and actions. To achieve personal growth, it really helps to have in mind some of the best affirmations that align with your goals and dreams.

The truth is that we are what we think we are and by using affirmations you will have the power to be in full control of all your thoughts. This way you can direct them to focus on the things that are good for your general wellbeing. You, however, need to know that you can't only rely on thoughts and must work on transforming those thoughts into words and ultimately into actions.

The best thing is that the moment you affirm your dreams and desires you will be empowered with a sense of reassurance that your words will become your reality. The thing is, when you think of all your desires - your thoughts will create your reality. Explained below are important affirmations for your personal development that I believe will be of so much help:

My failures are a learning experience

Affirming to this every day gives you a different approach towards failure and helps you know that failure does not mean you are not good enough. The most successful individuals are those who understand that it is through failure that we grow and also through failure that we achieve great things.

I create value in my own life

This reminds you of your responsibility to always make yourself better in all ways and focus your efforts on doing things that only add value to all areas of your life.

I have what it takes to be a success

The truth is that we all have so much potential within us to achieve greatness, but if you lack this awareness, then you won't go far in life. As a person, it really helps to remind yourself every day that you actually have what it takes, and you will never give up on your dreams.

I appreciate myself and where I am in life

It is through self-love and appreciation that individuals can attain real success and happiness in life. This, therefore, means that self-appreciation makes you view the world differently and will help you approach life with more confidence and bravery.

I am very hard working

Apart from positive thinking, hard work comes in as a major factor in achieving goals and dreams. It is therefore very essential to remind yourself every day how hard working you are, and you will end up being exactly that.

My life is changing for the better

This affirmation is meant to help you be the kind of person who embraces change and does not allow any challenges or obstacles deter them from growing. It is also helpful in giving you the realization that your life is changing and that you are doing good work on that.

Chapter 10: The Power Of Belief

"In any project the important factor is your belief. Without belief there can be no successful outcome." William James

You may not be aware of it but your beliefs are responsible for the outcome of your life. If you believe that you will fail, chances are that you will. You are lining yourself up for failure and saying to the world:

"Pick me! Pick me! I want to be a failure."

Although you may not see things in that way, that's exactly what is happening to many people who do not fulfill their full potential. Remember, I quoted the placebo effect in the last chapter. Those who took dummy medications and who believed that they would work actually improved their medical outcome. The power of belief is everything.

In your journal, I want you to write down some things you would like to change about yourself or about your life. There is a very specific purpose for this. Just the simple act of writing down our goals and aspirations can have a powerful effect on us. It's hard to get where you want to go if you don't have a plan and don't know the way there. Seeing your goals in written form helps to keep them in the forefront of your mind, therefore beginning the process of telling yourself a different story, much like the affirmations we'll talk about later on. Over time you will begin using an alternative way of thinking. From now on you'll have the tools to begin moving your life in a much more positive direction.

What you believe, you will live. If you believe that you are a failure, you will become a failure, though you need to know that the power of the mind is such that it writes your life story. If you want the story to have a happy ending, you have to write it in your mind. Remembering that the mind listens to negative thoughts more than positive ones, we have to boost the positivity in your mind so that it pushes the negativity into obscurity.

What's the first word that comes into your mind when you want to describe your life? I have used this question with many people and usually it's a negative word. It may be:

- Boring
- Difficult
- Lonely
- Lacking
- Average
- Unfulfilled

The reason why all of your descriptions border on negative is because that's the way your mind has been programmed to think over the course of your lifetime. If you beat yourself up every time something goes wrong, remember, your subconscious mind is recording your reactions to life and assumes these to be normal. The difference between the subconscious and the conscious mind is that the subconscious mind doesn't put emotions into the equation. It simply believes what you are telling it and, the more you think on something, the stronger those thoughts get. Thus, it becomes more and more ingrained.

What scientists have found out about the subconscious mind is that the series of habits that form your life is what is being recorded, but by changing those reactions to given stimuli you can actually change your future reactions. For those trying to add positivity to their lives, this tool is a very valuable one. Just as the neurons working together make your mind a very powerful tool in your life, the reaction of the subconscious mind is equally as important. Thus, if you can make yourself aware of habits that may be impeding on your own happiness, you can physically change them and rewrite the information hard-wired into your subconscious.

I think it's amazing that there is so much scope to the mind and that it's tapped into simply by changing life habits. For example, your choice of friends will have an impact on your beliefs. Mix with people who are negative and your view of life becomes equally negative. Mix with those who have a positive influence on your life and you begin to see a difference in the way that you perceive the world to be.

The worst habit that human beings have is negative talk. This doesn't mean that you always say negative things to other people, but it does mean that you use negativity within the confines of your brain when directing thoughts toward yourself. If you regularly tell yourself how unfulfilled your life is, your subconscious mind assumes this is true. The outcome is that your life becomes unfulfilling. However, think how powerful your life will become when you feed the mind positive and energizing feedback. The Law of Attraction works on the basis that you attract to your life that which is in line with your thoughts. Thus, if you think like a pauper, you will always be one. However, if you start to open up your thinking, the power of belief in life and in yourself can open up avenues you never thought possible.

There are some wonderful opportunities waiting for you in your life and yet, day in and day out, you feed yourself limiting beliefs. Now is the time to start to look at life from a different viewpoint because, when you do, everything changes.

Chapter 11: Positive Energy Techniques

Are you unsure of what way you should feel about a situation? If so, you are creating negative energy. Even if you are just uncertain about "how" positive you should be, this creates a negativity. Sadly, when we create negative energy it brings our beliefs, our opinions and our overall mentality down with it. I used to regularly be the one to kill a room of positive thinking and action with negativity. Foolishly, I used to look at it as "realism"!

However, I was informed of this negativity by my brother, Joe. Joe told me it was a disgrace how I could ruin the positivity in a room, and that I had to fix this part of my mentality immediately. Obviously, I felt threatened by this and wanted to do something to try and change that opinion of me.

So, I looked into how I could reverse the transaction. In my mind I would turn a positive room into a negative one – so how could I go about doing the opposite?

I had to take a look at what the underlying fears that led me to negative thinking was being produced by. By simply taking a moment to see what feelings were creating that negativity, I found it much easier to escape from. By simply questioning where the negativity came from, I could very quickly take that negativity and turn it into positivity. This works simply by not wanting to be negative – as soon as I can make myself aware of that negativity, I fight back against it. All it takes is being able to think about the subject in a new way.

The easiest way to change your mindset and get you out of a cyclical way of thinking (do you ever find you just keep repeating the same problems in your head?) is to engage in a hobby. Find something that you enjoy doing, and use that to change your mindset. When we engage in an activity that we enjoy, it makes us more likely to take a positive approach to other subjects floating around in our brains.

So, by simply taking a quick break from the repeated negativity in the mind, I can take the positive energy that this creates. My time spent enjoying that hobby allows me to take that negative build-up, and make it positive. Now, when I return to thinking about the issue that was bringing me down, I can re-frame the idea and make it more positive.

The easiest way to generate positive energy simply comes from looking at how you can help others, too. Whatever the problem you are creating negative energy worrying about, you have a way to correct this issue. Rather than looking at why this situation is going to create a burden for you specifically, re-frame it as why this situation could be used to help someone else. That creates positive energy, and makes us feel better.

Positive energy creation takes time, but it's made simpler with a basic re-adjustment of our thoughts! Now, let's look at how some people are capable of "training their brain" to avoid negativity.

Chapter 12: Practice Gratitude

Being grateful is one of the most generous actions anyone can make. As simple as it may sound, our minds may be so cluttered that we cannot take the moments to appreciate everything that we have. It may easy to list off as many things going wrong with our life, but how about listing everything good in life? There are millions of things that each one of us can feel grateful about. The life we live, your ability to read, the air we breathe, everything!

You can use your journal to help you. When you wake up write down three things that you are grateful for and continue to do so until it becomes part of your daily morning routine. I guarantee you that becoming gracious will change your life perspective on life. By doing this simple ritual even a person who has lived life with mediocrity will feel blessed and fortunate.

Nothing in life is to be taken for granted. Every little thing has infinite value and we honor this value by becoming grateful for it. Simply having a life is worth being grateful for. Be thankful for people and for your possessions.

The minute we become thankful and satisfied with what we have and with who we are, we can envision an even brighter future with even more opportunities to be thankful.

Here are some more practical advice on how any one person can become a deeply grateful compassionate human-being. Here are the things that are required to become a very powerful force of nature and genuinely gracious at all things life must offer:

Make a commitment to yourself

You need to set a goal for yourself for improvement and commitment to practice becoming a thankful person to the people and things that make up your life. When you wake up in the morning, you should boldly declare to yourself, "I am going to be grateful today."

Gratitude is not a subconscious decision, but you can habitually train your mind to become gracious at everything that you do. Gratitude is a conscious decision. You must practice it consistently for it to soak deep inside your mind. Now for example, if you have a coworker just willing to pick up an item you've dropped, that's a luxury some people don't have and you should go out of your way to thank them.

Know the value of others around you

We all want to be treated and acknowledge substantially at work, so why not give it to others? To become grateful, you must know the value of others and things in life. For example, it is very easy to forget the value of your coworkers. But they have the same working life as you. You may have already implanted this mindset that "it's their job to be a good worker". However, it's their choice.

If you wish for your life to become more thrilling then pay respect for each small acts of kindness that comes to them, whether it's assistance on their duties, an enlightening compliment, or just being there for them.

Help other people and do good deeds

A practicable approach to gratitude is to practice giving and spreading positivity to the world around you, this can ensure a much better world. Now, many religions and cultures value the fact of helping others and positive energy. By doing these random acts of kindness, it will be repaid to you by a better understanding to the world. Helping others goes a long way. It can make you feel more superior, restore the joys of life, and make people believe that there is hope in humanity.

Goodness pays back equally. Though you should never do something good just because you want to gain something in life. Here are some ideas of how you can give positive energy and help others around your workplace:

1.   Pay compliments

2.   Ask if you can help your coworkers with anything

3.   Volunteer to work overtime

4.   Smile more

5.   Hold the door for others

6.   Write a thank you note for someone whose been working hard

7.   Buy a gift for your boss and fellow coworkers

8.   Eliminate negativity

It is very easy to be absorbed by our own personal goals and development. But by stepping outside of our daily routines and comfort zones to just help someone, it will provide amazing perspective and insight to fill up your working place with only positive energy.

Stop Comparing Yourself with Others

Many people often compare themselves with others, some of us may not even be fully aware that we are comparing ourselves with our coworkers. However, the comparison is only depriving us of the joys of life. With us always saying to ourselves that "Are they better than me."

we lower our self-esteem and make us feel bad about ourselves. You must resist the urge to compare boy self with others.

Why would you compare yourself to others, when you are one out of a million? No one else will look like you, think like you, or be you. No one can build themselves up to be exactly like you. Life is about being the bet you possibly can be, not about being the best in the world and certainly not about being someone you are not. Resist the urge to compare yourself, and you will find great gratitude in yourself.

Instead, you should rather compare yourself to yourself. Think of yourself as the only person you need to compete with. To put to an example, don't compare yourself to how successful you are than your friends, ask yourself if you are more successful than you were last year. Make progress in your life, and which can only

be done by not comparing yourself to the
many people around you.

Chapter 13: Start At One

When you have made up your mind to do something, it is natural to want to start it as soon as possible. However, trying to do everything at once will only set you back and make you feel negative when you have to deal with the disappointment of not making changes 'fast enough'. Thus, the need to start small and then build up from there; starting small is the best way to get rid of negative thinking and build a habit that will allow you to embrace positivity. Changing your mindset does not happen overnight.

Yes, the realization for the need to make changes may come to you in a 'eureka' moment, but you may have been feeling down for a long time, which means you need to work hard to make changes. Unfortunately, the thought of working hard can stress you out. This is why you need to start developing small effortless habits that seem 'too small' not to make.

For example, if you are always searching for your keys in the morning, you can put a hook near the door and endeavor to place your keys there once you get into the house. This seems like a small thing to do but if you do so, you will save the minutes you usually spend looking for your keys in the morning.

Once you adapt to the new habit, you can move on to the next habit you want to develop. The purpose of developing such habits is so to make your life easier and less stressful. Therefore, you need to look at your life and determine the little things you do that make a difference on how you feel at the end of the day.

One thing that can help you keep sight of the changes you need to make is setting goals. The goals you set can be as small as you want them to be. Even though they may appear small now, eventually they will add up and enable you to have a more positive outlook in life.

Chapter 14: Replacing Negative With Positive

The simple conscious act of recognizing negative thoughts is where this journey to happy begins. Many of us repeat negative statements in our heads or even engage in complaint filled conversations.

If you were to make a note of it every time you thought something negative, or made a negative comment, or engaged in a negative conversation, you would be able to fill a notebook a day.

Noticing negative thoughts when they occur is one way to begin taking control of your happiness. Each time a negative thought comes to mind, tweak it...give it a positive spin or engage in a positive behavior.

You will get better and better at this the more you practice. Your goal is to notice as many negative thoughts as you can and make them positive.

Each time you replace a negative thought with a positive behavior or thought you are sending a signal to your subconscious.

The more you do this, the quicker your subconscious will begin to focus on the positive thoughts.

You are building a bridge between your conscious and autonomic nervous system.

How to Stop a Negative Thought

• When the thought occurs say the word stop in your head. Disrupt the thought as soon as it surfaces, breaking the chain of thought with the word stop will help you keep negativity at bay.

• Rationalize the negative thought when it surfaces, why do you think this?

What triggered the thought in the first place?

• Write it down, get a journal and write down your negative thoughts. Read through your journal and rationalize the thoughts and behaviors. Break down negative assumptions and write down any new positive understandings you have realized.

Replacing a negative thought before it becomes a negative behavior is the best outcome. When a negative thought arises, it can trigger a negative behavior, for instance; you know you have to speak in front of your colleague'stomorrow, you tell yourself,"I hate speaking in front of crowds, I am so awkward."

Telling yourself you don't like to speak in front of crowds because you are awkward is not a true statement.

You may feel awkward, but you arenot awkward, you wouldn't have a job where you have to speak to a crowd if you were truly awkward.

Be truthful and construct a new thought,"speaking in front of crowds makes me feel awkward"is not as discouraging as the first thought.

The more you recognize and catch those negative thoughts, the more adept you will become at replacing them with positive, encouraging thoughts and statements.

Write down those negative thoughts and when you have time, read through them and re-write them in a more accurate and truthful way.

You will be pleasantly surprised how quickly this exercise begins to change your thought patterns.

When we are stressed, it seems like blowing off steam is the best way to feel better. The truth is, if you are blowing off steam by complaining and exaggerating the situation, you are only adding to the negativity. The best way to"blow off steam"is to go and do something you enjoy, do something positive.

You can replace the negativity of the day with positive thoughts and emotions by engaging in an activity that you enjoy.

Ranting about negative things that happened during the day won't help you feel better...doing something you enjoy will replace the negative with a positive...end your day on a happy note.

Positive affirmations and a positive self-image play an important part in achieving happiness. The cliché, "if you don't love yourself, you can't love someone else" is true.

If you have a poor self-image, the positive emotions that bond a people together are not readily available. Positive affirmations will only get you so far, you need both to achieve happiness.

Positive affirmations are uplifting, supportive, statements that will help you attain a positive self-image.

Achieving and maintaining a positive self-image requires self-respect and self-love. Write down 5 of your best qualities, then read them off to yourself. Keep these 5 qualities in the forefront of your mind and call on them when you are feeling bad about yourself.

The easiest way to find some positive affirmations is to look them up on the internet. There are millions of quotes available online, spend some time researching positive affirmations and quotes, then write down your favorites and keep them in your journal.

These affirmations are a way for you to express how you feel about yourself.

Whenever stress gets you down, or you are having a bad day, spend a few minutes reading through your positive affirmations, they will help you fight the negativity. Never be to harsh or beat yourself up when things don't go as planned. Remember, you only want what's best for yourself, you are not the enemy.

The more time you spend focusing on positive thoughts and feelings, the less time you have to pay attention to negativity.

Bad things happen, things don't always go your way, but, these things only have power over your life if you give them that power.

It's ok to acknowledge mistakes, it is not ok to call them failures. Mistakes can motivate you to new heights of achievement instead of dragging you under and drowning you in failure.

Simple Tips to Remember

•   Stop negative thoughts the moment they rise to the surface...Stop!

•   Rationalize your negative thoughts, talk to yourself...ask yourself why?

•   Write down your negative thoughts and feelings in a journal

•   Replace negative thoughts with positive behaviors, engage in something you enjoy

The more you actively work to change negative to positive, the more receptive your subconscious will become to positive associations and assumptions.

Negativity is subjective, your perception of situations, people, and things will change if you stop those thoughts and question them when they occur. Don't exaggerate negative perceptions of yourself, and be truthful with yourself.

Always accept responsibility for your actions, positive thinking is only effective if you are honest with yourself.

It can be difficult to identify negative thoughts and replace them with positive ones if you don't recognize your own responsibility.

Take the time to think your behavior through, and if you are to blame, accept it and move on. Denial only leads to more negative thoughts and actions, own it and let it go.

Chapter 15: The Pessimist

It is easier to solve a problem when you know what causes it. Aperson's stress or unhappiness is sometimes a result of his own perspective of himself, of others and of circumstances. Previously, we have learned that pessimists are dominated by negative thoughts. Several factors trigger these negative thoughts.

Fear is one thing. You have to understand that all sorts of emotions are natural in a human being, and fear is one of them. The big difference between positive and negative people is that the latter are clouded with fear, and this fear paralyzes them into thinking of options to overcome unpleasant situations. Fear and negative thoughts are interlocked. Fear causes negative thoughts; negative thoughts cause fear. You have to eliminate one to get rid of the other.

Stress is another. Unpleasant situations cause a lot of stress. Lack of belief in one's abilities as well as wrong or irrational thinking can also cause stress. Pessimists think like these:

(1) One minor incident can ruin everything. Example scenario: The whole morning was perfect when suddenly, he accidentally spilled coffee on his shirt. Because of one minor accident, he thought that his day will turn out to be a complete mess. He may overlook and forget all the good things that may happen throughout the day because of it.

(2) "It's always my fault. There is nobody to blame but ME."

(3) Always expecting the worst in everything.

(4) Everybody can do it, except me.

Example scenario: John wants to become a professional writer. A publishing company asked him to submit a 300-page compelling novel in order for them to sign him up. The manuscript is due in 6 months. In his mind, John thinks that 6 months is too short to write a very long novel. He thinks this is his only opportunity to get his dream job. He tries to write the first few pages. It took him almost a week. He went over his write-up, but felt that it was unsatisfactory. He thinks other writers can do better than him.

"Will I be able to finish this on time? Should I start from scratch? But I don't have enough time. I need something good or else..." All these thoughts made him more stressful and fearful. What would he do next? Let's get back to him later on.

Stress causes fear. Fear results to more stress, and all these can ruin one's happiness and chances of attaining success.

Chapter 16: Don't Sweat The Small Stuff

According to studies, people who frequently feel happy do not perform better than people who only experience happiness on occasion in terms of academic and career accomplishments. The reason for this is that constantly happy people are alright with foregoing a certain degree of success for happiness' sake. This might be the reason why some people label themselves as contented in the sense of simply settling. However, in their defense they have a different set of priorities compared to others.

To become a generally happy person does not mean you should slack off on your responsibilities. It simply means you should let go of perfectionism. Avoid paying too much attention to the little details, and instead, step back and take a look at the bigger picture.

For instance, if you and your friend are working on a report and he forgets to add a particular segment, you can choose to just let it roll off your back instead of entertaining feelings of frustration. Count to ten then consider if that segment is crucial to your report. If it is, then you can inform your friend about it in a neutral manner, so the two of you can work something out. If it isn't as important, then there is no point in dwelling.

Happiness Exercise: Every now and then, we face little details that might irritate us, which are actually not as important and significant in our lives. To help train your mind to shrug off these unnecessary causes of stress, start by asking yourself this question: "Will this affect my life significantly?" If your answer is still yes, then remind yourself that any problem can be solved with proper planning and timing, as long as you do not let worry get in the way.

Next, take deep breaths and ask yourself this second question: "What can I learn from this?" If these little details will not contribute to your growth and learning anyway, then there is definitely no point in lingering on them.

Finally, ask yourself this: "Will the world end because of these problems?" Remember that everyone has problems, and these problems are just a part of life. Another question that you can ask yourself is, "Will this matter a century from now?" Most likely, no one will even remember insignificant details ten years from now, much less a hundred.

Positive Affirmation: To help set your mind in the right mood whenever you are faced with problems, here are some great positive affirmations you can tell yourself:

"I choose to be happy and focus my mental energy only on what matters the most."

"Slow down, take a deep breath, and take it easy."

"I know for a fact that this too shall pass."

You can even go right ahead and print out the positive affirmation of your choice in big bold letters. Hang it on a wall in your work space or put it in your bedroom for you to see every day. Let it be a gentle reminder to yourself that your problem is not all it is cracked up to be, and life will surely take a turn for the better once you accept that you cannot win them all.

Chapter 17: Exercises To Control Your Thoughts

Now you know the simple methods to get out of negativity. But there are some exercises which if done regularly can lead to greater control of your own mind and a life filled with positivity.

Meditation

Meditation is by far the best way to control your mind. For example, mindfulness meditation involves focusing on your breath and being mindful of what goes in your mind without any judgment. Just breathe deep, let thoughts come, observe them, and gently return to your breath. Latest research shows that meditation changes the brain structure with neuroplasticity. It means that new pathways are built and your brain learns relaxed ways of reacting to difficult situations.

Practicing meditation for the long-term increases the gray matter in the brain, which is responsible for self-referential processing. This means you'll be better able to make decisions being in tune with your emotions. Meditation shows concrete results after 4-8 weeks and you'll feel amazing when negative thoughts won't be able to haunt you anymore. Below is a simple meditation technique that you can practice.

How to Meditate

It is important that you find a suitable room or place to meditate. The place needs to be quiet and free from any kind of distraction. Ensure that your phone is off and you will not have any kind of distractions. It is also important that you choose a suitable time to meditate when you will be relaxed and not aggravated, as this will make meditating hard. Also wear loose clothing.

Before you start to meditate, it is important that you choose a suitable period that you want to meditate. If you are new to meditating, you can start with 5 minutes.

1. Sit in a chair comfortably with hands on your lap. Ensure your neck is relaxed and chin tucked in.

2. Close your eyes then take deep breaths; breathe in through your nose, and out through your mouth.

3. Notice your body sensations as your body touches the chair and your feet touch the ground and feel your arms resting on your legs.

4. Scan your body from head to toe and take note of any discomfort or tension. Don't try to change anything just notice it.

5. Now turn to your thoughts and notice any thought arising without attempting to change them are making any judgment.

6. Turn your focus back to your breath, the rising and falling of your chest and how you feel each time you inhale.

7. Let your mind be free by spending just 20-30 seconds sitting there feeling calm.

8. Now become aware of your physical feelings of the chair beneath, and even your feet making contact with the floor and your arms on your lap. Notice any smells, tastes or any other feelings.

9. Count from 5 to 1, open your eyes and go on with your daily activities.

Journaling

Journaling helps you look at your situation from a distant perspective and know more about yourself in general. When you write about your day and your feelings everyday, you'll get to know what matters to you and what is frivolous. You'll get to know your dreams, the people whom you love the most and the places you want to go. Journaling is like having a friend who is ready to listen to your endless rants, not raising an eyebrow when you go over the board. The more you write down your feelings and experiences, the more you notice a pattern of, for instance, negative thinking at a certain time and once you do this, you can make the necessary changes to change your thinking.

How to Journal

There are two approaches to journaling. One is when you are experiencing too much negativity that it is putting you off focus from your daily routine. The other is routine journaling, which you might want to do everyday before going to sleep.

When you experience a problem, always try to keep it short while writing or you'll do more harm than good. Define the problem and try to find possible solution.

When you do routine journaling, just do it like you are keeping a memoir of the events of the day. For example, a get together with your old friends might have made your day. Write all the small things.

Practicing Gratitude

When the Hollywood actor Matthew Mcconaughey was awarded an Oscar for

Best Actor, he first wanted to thank God. And he said, "God has given me opportunities that are not of my human hand. He has made me realize that it is a scientific fact that truly, gratitude reciprocates."

So how can you be grateful? Just write in your journal or a sheet of paper, the things you have in your life, which you feel grateful for. And remember you don't need to have a BMW to be grateful. Just being able to breathe alone is something to be grateful. There are some people lying in hospital beds on machine unable to breathe. Just having friends and a family that love you is something to be grateful. Be grateful even for the job you have even if you don't like it because there are some people who have no source of income.

Giving

A certain joy comes from giving. How do you normally feel when you give your time, money, or effort? In most cases, you feel good and great about yourself; thus, generating positive energy. Therefore, if you want to feel good about yourself, give to the society. Spend some time in an orphanage or senior homes. You will come out of there grateful for what you have and happy for what you have contributed. The more you do this, the more positive thoughts and energy you have and the harder it will be to have negative thoughts.

Visualizing

"It's the possibility of having a dream come true that makes life interesting."

- Paulo Coelho

Many leaders have regarded visualization as a powerful tool to achieving success. When you visualize yourself doing what you always wanted to do, you get a surge of energy, which makes you believe that it might be actually possible. Our thoughts have more power than we know. Everything in this world that has ever been made is because a person thought about it at some point in their lives.

So how does visualizing make you become more positive? The more you visualize about your dream, the more real it seems and the more you will think it is possible to achieve that dream and with this, there is no room for negativity because you are concentrating on achieving your dreams and not on negativity.

Chapter 18: Imagination: Our Creative

Ability

Imagination allows us to look at every situation from a different perspective, using our minds we can mentally explore the past and the future.

Day Dreaming is one of most well-known form of imagination. Day dreaming to a certain degree might bring temporary happiness and relief stress.

Anything is possible with imagination you can get anywhere quickly; travel without barriers and beyond the obvious physical limitations. You can feel free, even temporarily and only in your mind can you be set free from all fears, all life challenges, all negative self-talk and unpleasant circumstances.

The imaginative power covers all five senses, emotions and feelings that one can experience.

We can imagine everything from smells, tastes, sounds to feelings and emotions. For some, it is much easier to see images of the mind (mental pictures) while others find it even easier to imagine certain feelings.

Professional training of the power of imagination gives us the opportunity to combine all the senses.

That is why in this chapter, I will give you a full complete training and you too can experience the wonders of this hidden secret. You need imagination to develop positive thinking.

A strong creative imagination does not make one a mere day dreamer.

Actually, it increases your creativity ability and is the best tool for recreating your world. That's why imagination is often referred to as our creative ability.

Imagination can shape your life, believe me. This is usually done by creating creative visualization together with affirmations.

It is the force behind the creation of the circumstances, dreams and events in your life. If you know how to work with it, you can make the desires of your heart and your dreams come true.

The reason for this chapter is to show you exactly what to do.

We all need a dose of imagination in our lives. It has a great role and the value to keep us alive and kicking.

It is way beyond just idle daydreaming as some people suppose. Even though we are not aware, we experience its power in our daily lives consciously or unconsciously.

Think of mundane things such as planning a wedding, vacation trip or a meeting.

We use it when we describe an event to give instructions, to write stories and it was used in the movies we watch. Do you know that even music the result of imagination?

It is an important part of creative visualization, affirmations and positive thinking.

Hidden secret: The display of an object or a situation in our minds and repeating this mental image as often as possible attracts the object or situation we visualize into our lives.

This is why most people are sick because their minds were concentrated on their fears of getting sick. This opens up new, large and fascinating possibilities.

We can do anything and achieve anything as far as our imaginative eyes can see. What you see is what you get.

Always think in a positive way towards your dreams, lest you attract into your life situations events circumstances and people you don't really want.

Thoughts: are pictures of the mind with constructive and destructive meaning.

If the power of imagination is not properly used, we may wonder why bad things are happening to us. This is actually what most of us face.

Bad things happen to good people; it's all in your way of thinking, it's all in the power of imagination.

If you choose to under-estimate the power of imagination, you may run the risk to living a stressful, unhappy, worried, and unsuccessful life.

People commit suicide because they under-estimated the power of imagination. It all started from the mind, the negative thoughts combined with negative self-talk.

Exactly what to do!

Always stay in the right mind-set, think positively and expect success. Never expect the worst case scenario and if not, do not think or believe that fate is against you.

You are fully responsible for your life and nothing changes with time, if you see things not going where you want them to go, turn around and take charge of the power of imagination by developing a positive attitude, then life will automatically brighten and unfold for you.

A clear understanding on how to make a positive use of your imagination and implement this knowledge for your own benefit and other people will set you on the golden road to success, fulfilment, satisfaction and happiness.

Chapter 19: The Secret

Standing Up & Being Counted

So, the next part that I want to take a look at comes down to the power of negativity once again. One major problem that I have faced in the past is not being able to take responsibility. It ties in with the above quite well, hence why I wanted to bring it up now and let you know what the long-term aim here is: I want to help make sure that, come the end of this book, you feel comfortable taking responsibility. For negative thinkers, taking any kind of responsibility is a very challenging thing to go through with.

Why? Because it means being negative about yourself even more. When you feel like you are always on your own case, it can feel like a relief not taking responsibility. For once, you don't need to let someone else tell you how awful you are – you are already doing that as it is.

The most powerful transition that you can look to carry out, then, is going to come down to standing up and being counted when it matters most. This isn't meant that you need to wade in and be the knight in shining armour for the damsel in distress: it means taking your criticism and the challenges in life when they come to you.

If you want to be happier, then you have to be ready to take responsibility for when you fail. I used to look the other way, pretending that it was down to someone else why I had failed. It was never my fault, as I had enough on my plate and I couldn't cope with the idea of yet more failure. Instead of making me happier as I wrongly thought, I found that this inability to take responsibility meant that I was never learning. So, I was just making the same mistakes over and over, without fail.

I would walk into the same old mistakes, and keep having to avoid any kind of responsibility. It was easier to just pretend that it was down to someone else, and there was nothing that I could do, rather than admitting that I was culpable for the mistakes that I have made.

So, how do you go about taking responsibility? What is the easiest way to make sure that, at the end of this, you stand up and are willing to be counted?

First off, you have to want to be happier in the first place. If you still find yourself always looking for a means to blame yourself and to avoid taking any kind of responsibility, then you aren't quite ready to become a positive thinker yet. Only those who are willing to take responsibility and be treated with severity when they make a mistake can really turn to themselves and say that they are ready to be more positive.

Why? Because only those who are ready to be more positive are willing to listen to the criticism and to really handle the consequences of taking responsibility.

It's a major problem, and something that can leave many people unsure of where to turn to. I used to think that I was ready, until I would start listening to the music. Before I knew it, I was in court-room mode again, offering excuse after excuse to try and get the spotlight off me. I wasn't ready for third-party inspection and having to listen to the criticism of others and having to make changes to who I was.

Simply put, I was not mature enough to be able to make such a decision and live with the consequences.

Over time, though, I began to see a hypocrisy in this. Even at my most negative, I would hang around like a bad smell waiting for praise and positive reinforcement when I had done something right. I expected that gold star every time that I was not messing up, but would never hang around long enough to listen to the criticism that was sure to follow.

As you can imagine, that created a negative and unhappy mentality that made it very hard for me to move on from who, and where, I was. Instead, I began to notice that if I was willing to hang around and take the positive vibes when I did things right, that I should be chasing that feeling more often instead.

So, I started to spend some more time looking at myself as someone who wanted to chase the long-term positive reinforcement by listening to the criticism. It was a simple change in looking at how I was being criticized, but it changed me from being totally unwilling to listen to completely ready to start seeing how I could chase the positive feeling of progression.

Rather than shirking the fear of being told that I wasn't good enough or that I had messed up, I looked to chase the eventual positive glow that I would get when I made the changes that were being asked of me, regardless of the challenge.

It's a subtle mentality shift, but it was so important for me to start making a progressive change to the way that I looked at the world around me as a whole. Now, rather than always looking to only get the good when I did things right first time, I looked to take a more progressive approach!

I started to look more for the praise after a period of progressive change. Rather than seeing the critique of my failure in the past as a personal assault, I started to see it as a new challenge - as constructive critism It was a small shift in the way that I allowed my mind to work, but it was a vital way to start looking at things, I believe. Without that, I would have very much continued to stay stagnant in my improvement as a person as well as a professional. This made such a huge difference to how I felt. Now, let's take a look at the next Secret to positivity!

Chapter 20: Don't Run Away From

Fear

After accepting that you are accountable for your happiness and sadness, success and failures, you need to understand that you need to stop running away from your fears and giving in to them if you desire to pave way for your accomplishments and triumphs.

Understanding the Effect of Fear on Your Life

Fear has an extremely devastating effect on your personality and your life. When you become fearful of doing something, you start limiting yourself. You lack belief in yourself and your potentials, which is why you give in to your fears. And when you begin succumbing to your fears and the different challenges of your life, you are unable to move on. You never find out what your true potential was and whether or not you would have defeated that challenge. All you know is to live a life full of fears.

Moreover, another important thing you need to know about fear is that it is a choice that you make. Whenever you encounter a difficult situation, you have two ways to tackle it. First, you could face it and ultimately learn the way to overcome it. Secondly, you could avoid it to escape it. If you choose the second, you are able to avoid experiencing the difficult situation for the moment, but the fear attached to it begins growing and strengthening. Hence, choosing fear is synonymous to choosing a life full of troubles. If you really want to move ahead in life and learn the way to become successful, you need to stop running away from your fears and start being brave. When you become fearless, you start believing yourself. This helps reinforce your self-esteem and confidence, which gives you the courage to take risks, overcome your fears and experiment in life. When you do all of that, you are able to discover new ways to succeed in attaining your objectives and becoming truly and totally happy and successful.

'Only when we are no longer afraid, do we begin to live.'- Dorothy Thompson

If you want to be bold, fearless and successful, here's what you need to do.

Believe You Can Do it

To become brave, you need to first practice self-belief. You need to tell yourself that challenges will come and go, and you'll always face a new situation that will make you go weak in the knees. However, if you believe that you can face and overpower that situation, you will be able to proceed forward, otherwise you are going to stay stagnant and this fast-paced, ruthless world doesn't treat the motionless with much respect and care. Therefore, you need to commit yourself that from this day onwards, you are going to face your fears. For that, you need to visualize facing your phobias and envision that you conquer them beautifully. Think of this scenario for 10 minutes daily with great conviction and within days, you would have found the courage to face your fears.

Take Small Steps

Once you feel you have the strength to face the things and situations you dread the most, you need to begin taking baby steps. Remember, you have just managed to become courageous, so taking big leaps is not wise at the moment. You need to get started by making small changes, so you can move gradually and ultimately overpower your fears. If you are afraid of taking risks in your business, then first you need to find out all the risks that you can take which can help your business grow. Next, you need to implement the smallest risk with the least side-effects and once it pays off, you can gradually move on to taking bigger risks.

Make sure to always keep moving; yes, there will be times when you will feel you lack the ability to go further and conquer the challenge, and it is okay to waver once in awhile. After all, you're only human. What's important is that you don't take an incredibly long hiatus and step up after a little while. Once you make bravery a constant trait of your personality, you will never give up and will always discover new ways of being happy and prosperous.

Chapter 21: Positive Thinking And

Your Career

In most work places, we find ourselves tempted to fall prey to gossip, political activity, climbing the corporate ladder and getting ahead. Yes, some work places are more harmonious than others and some industries more so, however being human means it is often tough to not allow the problems into your mind. As much as human resources management may be a function in a workplace that mediates and assists disputes and hiring processes, it is not a system that quantifies human worth, human function and most importantly human potential.

So what can you do, if you feel that you are living, loving, and breathing human being caught up in a cold, unloving and clinical workplace that completely lacks any heart and milk of human compassion? Is it even possible to change mindset and learn to enjoy the moment, instead of laboring miserably and feeling as if you want to keel over dead every morning, before you even head to work?

Here are a few thoughts and reflections to consider that will help you on your way:

Do not get emotionally attached to systems that you cannot change

By all means, be dynamic in a work environment. That means that you get up, show up, be interested and lively and contribute to the best of your ability within that space. Be the authentic professional you. However there comes a time when you also have to view the goings on of an environment through a rational lens.

So the boss may come into a meeting and rant and rave for a few minutes, particularly because of poor performance in a department. Maybe sales figures have gone down and the finance department is simply not happy. Whatever the case is, it is easy to get your stomach in knots over such a thing and carry mental strain.

Maybe you spent all weekend working hard on a presentation only to come in on a Monday morning and have it and your heart torn to pieces in the boardroom. Whatever the case may be, there are many moments where we all have felt 'less than' in a working environment.

Learn to detach your emotional involvement and self-worth from such situations. Know that to a great extent there is always a bigger picture and vision and you are there to facilitate an end goal, rather than reinvent the wheel. Surely, you listen to this piece of advice and think, yes that is easier said than done. Here are some practical ways on how you can learn to do so.

Cultivate other interests

Be a well-rounded person. Know that there is so much more to life than waging war at a work place and the confines of an office wall. In terms of relaxation, remember the feeling of sand beneath your feet and the grass between your toes. When things get too lofty and convoluted it helps to remember what it is like to be connected to the earth and something that is as elemental and trustworthy as the ground beneath your feet. Do you like to paint, blog, do design work, are you secretly cultivating an aviary in your spare time or nurturing bonsai plants secretly on the weekends?

As you cultivate other interests, you become more interesting. Your world view changes, you become a richer and more diverse and dynamic person to deal with. All of the pressure of who you are and what you are about in the workplace splits focus as you are able to converse about a number of different topics and experiences. People notice passion that is not being faked. People respond to heart, to excitement and authenticity. Unearth that in yourself and bring it to the table. You are worth it.

Get about the business of 'you'

Speaking about cultivating this of range of interests, what stops you from gradually turning your passion into your profession? If you feel so inclined, it is time to take things to the next level.

All of those popular internet sayings that relate to you not building your profession but others hiring you to build theirs actually does give quite a bit of food for thought. Current times, job markets, recessions and currency fluctuations calls on every individual not just to be a skilled member of the job sector, but to also call upon and develop their inner entrepreneur.

Do some market research, use the positive power of social media to build communities and raise interest around topics that are close to your heart and personal skills and services that you are trying to develop. Put 'numero uno', yourself at the heart of every business building exercise that you develop. It is time to get about 'the business of you.'

Invest energy in human relationships

It might seem like doom and gloom wherever you look at your workplace. It is easy to see cloak and dagger and smoke and mirrors, however, if you look closely enough, you may see a glimmer of humanity in somebody's eyes.

Look for that spark of humanity, find it, and cultivate it in whichever manner you see fit. It is easy to be ticked off with people and resolve not to try, but what progress will that ever bring?

Think about it, on a larger scale of things. How would peace ever be brokered between war torn countries, agreements be made, mergers developed and new inventions come to being without the wonderful interfacing and reacting of people?

Love, ideas, progress, innovation and many other things and ideas that come to be, only do so because people had the courage to get up and actually get about the business of communicating with other people. So the question is, who can you reach out to today?

Know your limits

Let's call it the influence of media that has gotten us to think that we are supposed to be industrious little hamsters on a wheel of everlasting activity until we can be taken seriously in the industry. On the other hand some of you may be suffering the indoctrination of watching movies in which we see interns starting off in the industry eager to please, doing everything from preparing the CEO's lunch, fetching their laundry to doing the office coffee run. Stop.

It is easy to consume media and think that unless you are a non-stop bustling, working wonder that the world will come to a standstill. While that may be useful when you're starting out your career, it isn't a type of thinking that will serve you well as you continue on your journey.

It is up to you to know when you're burning out, understand that as a human being, you are not an infinite resource. You need time to recharge, replenish and most importantly, you need to know what your limits are. If you are in fact unable to share that with the world, then prepare to become inundated with unreasonable requests that you will allow and that will simply leave you depleted as you go along in this journey of life. Learn to say no, set barriers and boundaries and show the world that you know who you are and what your value is.

Activate a switch

Once you know and understand your triggers, you are in an ideal place to know the signs and when to actually bail yourself out of such troubled situations. Have an escape route planned for when you feel that you are getting overwhelmed in life.

Take a walk outside, reach out to a friend, take the time to simply unplug and do something different. You come back completely revitalized and renewed.

Chapter 22: Positive Thinking And Health

If you are a positive thinker, your health is going to be better than a person who thinks negatively. This is because of the direct effect that our thoughts have on our hormones, the functioning of our organs and of course, the brain. Let us compare how positive and negative thoughts work on our body.

a. The effects of negativity

The problem with negativity is that it is an addiction of sorts. When you start to take comfort in negative thoughts, your head continues to fill up with them. This can have a serious impact on your physical and mental health and can even lead to behavioral changes.

An experiment conducted by the Journal of Personality and Social Psychology showed how negative thoughts can only make health issues worse than they already are. An experiment was conducted on college students who suffered from depression. Negative thoughts used to recur because of their current condition. However, when positive thoughts were induced these individuals were distracted from negativity.

Later in 2006, the Journal of Clinical Psychology published an experiment that was conducted on two groups. Group one consisted of people who were known to be anxious and Group two consisted of people who were not.

These two groups were asked to categorize several objects. When the criteria to categorize was obvious, both groups performed equally well. However, when the criteria became ambiguous, it was seen that the group of people who were prone to anxiety performed poorly.

Clearly, cognitive function was impaired with people who were prone to anxiety.

One of the most interesting studies with respect to thoughts and health was the effect of negative thoughts on pain. This study was published in the year 1990 and interestingly enough, it showed than with negative thoughts, pain sensations increased drastically.

The study was conducted on 185 subjects who suffered from sickle cell anemia, chronic pain and rheumatoid arthritis. The study aimed at understanding the effect of pain on negative thoughts and vice versa.

It was noticed that people who indulged in negative self-talk experienced a lot of pain in addition to mental stress. Those who suffered from chronic pain displayed more negative thoughts when pain flared up in comparison to those who suffered from sickle cell anemia and arthritis. The latter felt intermittent pain and did not display as many negative thoughts.

It is obvious that negative thoughts sprout when you feel pain. However, the more negative thoughts you allow in your mind, the more pain you are likely to feel. Mayo clinic says that the stress caused by negative thinking can cause havoc in your body. Some of the most common physical symptoms related to negative thinking are:

•	Digestive issues

•	Headaches

•	Muscle pain

•	Chest pain

•	Reduced sex drive

•	Insomnia or irregular sleeping patterns

•	Fatigue

•	Muscle tension

There are also several emotional symptoms such as:

•	Irritability

- Depression
- Lack of focus
- De-motivation
- Restlessness
- Mood swings
- Anxiety

These emotional and physical changes can have a big impact on your behavior and can even push a person to social withdrawal, substance abuse or alcohol abuse in the long run.

b. The effects of positivity

If thoughts have the ability to determine how healthy or unhealthy you are; and you are able to control thoughts, it only means that you can actually control health. Whether this is the truth or just a theory, the fact that there is a small possibility is certainly worth the try.

How does positivity affect your health?

It boosts your immunity

According to a recent study conducted on law students, it was observed that the immune response of the body became stronger when the students became optimistic. Immunity mediated by the cell was stronger, the WBC count improved drastically, helping the body cope against any infection easily.

This study also ruled out factors like genetics and personality that may affect health. The test categorized people based on their responses to questions related to goals and success. These were students that probably shared the same approach to life or had a similar personality at the very least. Then, their immune response was tested by injecting a very mild dose of candida yeast or dead mumps virus. They triggered an immune response which was a bump on the site of injection. The size of the bump showed how strong the immune response was.

Based on the exams and the progress of the academic year, the levels of optimism changed. When optimism increased, cell mediated response to germs improved and vice versa. It is believed that research like this can soon change the entire approach of treatment and counselling. While most of these treatments focus on the cause for stress or negative impact, inducing positivity and optimism could be the key to actually helping people deal with issues related to mental health.

Reduces risk of heart diseases

The heart, as we all know, is a very sensitive organ. It is very prone to diseases induced by extreme stress or anxiety. Sometimes, it can also be pushed to attacks or strokes with just the stress. It is true that people who eat better, exercise and make positivity a lifestyle lower the risk of any heart disease.

Close to 200 studies were revisited by researchers to understand the link between our behavior and the associated risk to heart diseases. Needless to say, research showed that people who were more optimistic were at a lower risk of developing cardiovascular diseases. It was noted by the popular journal, Psychological Bulletin that people who lived a happier life also chose a healthier lifestyle. They ate better food, slept well and also exercised more. As a result issues like cholesterol, blood pressure and obesity were lower in these subjects.

Close to 2800 patients who had already developed heart related conditions were followed by Duke University. Their observations stated that having a positive outlook reduced the chances of these diseases being fatal. The risk reduced by 50%!

When you have negative thoughts, your body is under a lot of stress. Sometimes, this stress translates as inflammations in your blood stream, leading to high chances of developing cardiac problems.

The good thing is that with some assistance, even if you are not an optimist naturally, there are coaching classes that can help you develop positive thinking. CBT or cognitive behavioral therapy helps you look at the positives in your life and induce this in you r life. Additional tools like music, book or even hobbies can help you improve your positive thoughts.

When the negative perspective is reduced, your heart health improves drastically because you are likely to improve the overall lifestyle that you follow.

More Resilience

When you undergo any sort of trauma or bad experience, it is likely to have an ill effect on your health. The faster you are able to bounce back from these negative experiences, the lesser you are prone to illnesses and diseases caused by this sort of trauma.

There are several factors that determine our response to trauma- our upbringing, the actual severity of the situation, etc. However, the most effective tool against trauma related health problems is the ability to induce positive self-talk and also improve your ability to think positively even in a difficult situation.

Longer life

A study was conducted by the University of London to prove that aging is a lot healthier in people who think positively. These people are likely to have any emotional or physical problems as they grow older. Of course, life expectancy increase in them, too.

This study was conducted on a group of men and women in the age bracket of 65 to 80 years. A simple questionnaire was used to assess their positive thoughts and optimism. Healthy aging was indexed using the scores from the physical health summary and also the feedback about these participants about their own health.

The thing with positive people is that they are likely to have more energy and more focus. That is why they are able to focus on following a healthier lifestyle than people who are negative or anxious. In this group, it was observed that people who were more optimistic were usually nonsmokers who indulged in regular physical activities. Optimistic people had something called positive health status, which made them want to be better in their overall health. This need to stay healthy was not affected by other factors like gender, overall body mass an even the clinical conditions that they suffered from.

It is obvious from these tests that people tend to age healthily when they are optimistic. Of course, the reduced levels of stress also ensure that the body is maintained in perfect harmony. With all the organs functioning at their best, the chances of age related illnesses are lesser.

These tests were conducted across the world with several parameters. The results were consistent to show that optimism is the primary factor in determining our aging process. The happier we are, the better we age. Of course, that also means a longer and happier life.

Tolerance to pain

In a study published by Science direct, it was proved that people who think positively have better tolerance to pain. We have seen in the previous section that with negative thoughts, response to pain becomes stronger.

A popular study was conducted on patients with mandibular disorders. The response to pain was measured in stressful and relaxed conditions. The stress was induced though verbal stressors. When ischemic pain was assessed in these conditions, it was noticed that optimism blunted the response to pain, allowing the person to cope easily. Those who were given verbal stressors not only showed less tolerance to pain, but also experienced more unpleasantness related to pain.

Reduces hypertension

One of the most common causal factors of heart diseases and several associated conditions is hypertension. A study was conducted to see if the levels of pessimism, optimism and anxiety had any effect on the ambulatory blood pressure and also if any effects on the cardiovascular system was moderated by the moods of a person. Adults with more anxiety and pessimism experienced higher blood pressure as expected in comparison to those with lower anxiety. Whenever the optimistic individuals of the group experienced negative emotions, their blood pressure rose significantly and actually matched the levels of the pessimistic individuals. With this study it became quite obvious that pessimistic thoughts had immediate and rather significant influences on the physiology and psychology of an individual.

When you think positively, you will be healthier as you have more energy to enjoy your life. This keeps you away from several habits that are detrimental to health, including overeating, substance abuse, alcohol abuse or even smoking.

When you make positive thinking a way of life, you will also realize that external situations do not affect you as much because you are able to keep your self-esteem high even in tough situations. When you are able to keep thinking positively about yourself, you are going to feel healthy and more interested in keeping yourself in good shape. When you love yourself, you do not mind investing in yourself. That includes following a good exercise routine, eating well and even pampering yourself regularly.

The good thing about positive people is that their relationships are healthy and positive. The more you are able to see the good in others, the easier it is for you to maintain good relationships. This of course means that you do not have the additional stress of managing your relationships and having to prove yourself all the time to people.

Chapter 23: How To Change The Odds

Of A Happy Life

LUCK—not the commonplace fortune-telling, Feng Shui or superstitious thing you think of—is largely the result of taking appropriate action. When you're passive, when you don't take charge of your affairs, you're a victim of all sorts of 'bad luck.'

When you permit yourself to accept bad luck there are usually reasons. You may feel that you can't or shouldn't take action. You may have unconscious fears. Or you may tend to blame society for things that go awry in your life. As some people say, it is the society that helps create the alcoholics, the drug addicts, the derelicts. But the truth is if one places the blame on others, it leads him or her away from looking within and facing up to his or her own part in what is going on.

Accepting bad luck also promotes passivity. For instance, if you continue to bring your childhood grievances, to feel overpowered by bad luck because everything is your parents' fault, you won't make any attempt to improve your lot.

When are you able to change your luck?

That's when you recognize your role in creating less-than-perfect situations. What determines your luck is how you make use of the resources, abilities (and disabilities) you've got. Remember what the great William Shakespeare has said, "The fault is not in our stars, but in ourselves."

One red flag that signals when to make a change is repetition. Take, for example, one woman who has had three unhappy marriages and sighs, "I'm so unlucky in love." Yet she forgets to realize that every man she picked had an alcoholic problem. When time and again you repeat frustrating failures in specific areas of your life, the piling up of undesirable outcomes often make you conclude that you have bad luck with those things.

Once you recognize a pattern of things going wrong, figure out your role and why you feel trapped in that situation. You ought to examine your excuses for wasting time and what actually lure you.

Oftentimes when you're anxious about things, you tend to push them out of your awareness: daydreaming about moving to a paradise island in the Caribbean, turning to alcohol, or going out and spending your money on unnecessary things. All of these actions deflect good luck.

Rather than running away from frustrating experiences in such manner, think of what can you do that will make you feel more competent. Forget about the drink or pointless telephone chat. Instead, make some small accomplishments, like doing a household chore you dislike such as cleaning a messy closet. In such way, you will promote new feelings of pleasure and security because you have pleased yourself that you have taken charge.

Making little changes makes you like yourself better, which in turn makes you start doing more useful things. Thus, you improve your life in small ways, which can lead to bigger ways. And that is your luck.

Chapter 24: Conduct A Self-Inventory

Conduct an honest self-inventory of your thoughts, emotions, and things that are important to you.

Do not be discouraged, bored, delay, or go slowly, for your success and happiness are at stake. Keep your mind focused on the many benefits you will enjoy if you achieve your goal.

This first step requires your full attention and cooperation. You need to make sure that everything will proceed according to your purpose.

Action Steps

Choose a private place and the right time to examine yourself without distraction.

You may use a notebook to list down things about yourself.

In one space, list down what you honestly think are your positive traits or habitual thoughts. In another space, list down the negative ones. Just use keywords for simplicity. Place similar traits or thoughts under one category.

Examples of positive traits are friendliness, helpfulness, generosity, honesty, and efficiency. Examples of negative traits are selfishness, laziness, disrespect, lying, and dishonesty. Thoughts proceed from traits. This exercise will try to reform negative thoughts and traits into positive ones.

Reflection

Changing one's outlook or way of thinking first requires knowing oneself as far as possible. Recognize your strengths and weaknesses honestly and objectively. You do not have to finish the self-inventory in one sitting, though. Your desire to succeed and to be happy will inspire you to perform this step, even if you find it difficult at first.

Chapter 25: Making It Part Of Your Life

The best way to become a master in any art and enjoy most of its best benefits is to learn as much as you can about that very art. Positive thinking is one of the most powerful tools one can possess and the best part is, it's all free!

It is possible you have allowed negative thinking to develop roots in your psyche perhaps because of negative circumstances you have had little or no control over. It could have also creeped into your mind through the teachings of others that may have mislead you into adopting a pessimistic mindset. Even if you have never practiced positive thinking in your life or learnt anything from this mental habit, below are tips you can adopt to master this all-important art starting today:

1: Read All Types of Literature That Emphasizes Optimism

There is a saying that learning happens not somewhere, but everywhere. There is no single blueprint on how to master the art of positive thinking. Over time, a little here and a little there will add up to make you a positive thinker. The sum of your experiences make up your identity and experiences. Let those things be filled with enlightening knowledge and figures that have changed this world for good.

Great authors have written a countless amount of magnificent books on positive thinking. The more of these books you can lay your hands on and digest, the more you will begin to adopt this practice, the science behind it, how it can better your life, and ways you can cultivate the positive mental attitude. Read it, understand it, and live it.

Books on mental shifts, positive mental attitude, positive mentality, and all other related topics can help you learn more about positive thinking as well as how to make it a part of your life. When you surround yourself with this kind of information, your mind subconsciously begins to believe and practice it.

2: Harness the Wealth of Information on the World Wide Web

The advent of the internet has simplified many aspects of life. Learning is one aspect of life the internet has made a whole lot easier and fun. With a simple click of your mouse, you can now access a wealth of vital and helpful information on virtually any topic.

There are blogs, websites, online forums, newsletters, webcasts, webinars, articles, eBooks, and social networks solely dedicated to helping you achieve a positive mental attitude and live the positive life of happiness and fulfillment. Connect with others seeking the same goal and strengthen each other to become the best version of yourselves.

Earlier in life when I was struggling with negative thoughts, self-talks, and beliefs, I relied on some of these sites and other online sources for daily inspiration and motivation. Some of these sites will help you understand the importance of practicing positive affirmations and speaking positivity into your day each morning before heading out.

3: Keep a Company of Friends Who Continually Motivate and Inspire You

One important way to learn more on positive thinking, is to hang out with people who have fought strong life battles and emerged victorious. The best people to learn positive thinking from are those who can share personal experiences on how the power of positive thinking has reshaped their lives and made life a whole lot more meaningful.

That friend who pulled through a life-threatening ailment can be a great source of inspiration in terms of how powerful a positive mental attitude can be.

That friend who recently came out of an abusive relationship or a divorce and still looks determined to find true love can help you learn how to use the power of positive thinking to turn the tides in your love life.

That friend who suffered a major business setback before striking great fortune will have one or two things to tell you about positive thinking.

That friend who lost all loved ones and properties to a natural disaster on manmade calamity and withstood the urge to attempt suicide can teach you elements of positive thinking.

Sometimes very insignificant events can help you become a positive thinker. Here is one of such minor events that shaped my positive thinking habit early in life:

The Little Football Fan Who Believed His Team Was Too Good to Lose

I cannot forget the great lesson I learnt about positive thinking and how it can help you stay happy even in the face of failure while expecting a better turn of events.

Back in high school, I went to a local football playing ground to watch a local match between two local football teams.

As I sat it an empty seat beside a calm little boy, I asked the boy about the score. He smiled and told me the other team was beating his team 3-0! I then questioned why he didn't look discouraged considering the fact that his team has obviously lost the match!"

The boy looked at me, smiled again and asked, "Why should I give up when the referee has yet to blow the final whistle" He looked at me in a puzzling way as if to say, "how can someone this big, lose faith in something so small?"

He told me he had faith in the team and the managers promised not to let him down. And as if by some miracle, the match ended 5-4 in favor of his team. It seemed like a story pulled straight out of a fairytale. Did he have control over the game? Most people would say absolutely not. But I believe that when someone believes hard enough, certain things just might happen.

It's fascinating how children as naïve as they are, can bring so much wisdom into our lives. That young boy taught me something that day. Sometimes, it is necessary to perceive life through the simple lens of a child. Be free of all complex factors and unnecessary burdens in life and just simply believe.

After that day, I came to see life with the faith and positive mentality similar to one that the boy was endowed with. I saw everything as a game where half time meant nothing; where it was never over until I said it was over; where temporary defeat did not equate to failure; where I would never blow my own final whistle when the referee had not even blown his. Simplify your life through this method, and you will find it is impossible to go through life gloomy and unhappy.

Chapter 26: How To Create A Happy

You

Happiness is and always will be, the most cherished yet most indefinable of all human emotions. Everyone searches for happiness, but many end the day with none.

Happiness cannot be given to you by another person and it is not something that we have permission to own. Happiness is simply a state of mind that is created by an individual.

Create more happiness in your everyday life with these 11 tips:

1. Reflect on your accomplishments

"There is joy in work. There is no happiness except in the realization that we have accomplished something." – Henry Ford

Everyday life passes us by, day-in day-out, often with little time to reflect on the things we have accomplished. However, everyone has done plenty of great things in their lives.

It doesn't matter if you're life isn't perfect right now. It's OK that you haven't quite reached your fitness goals, or that you're not at the top of your chosen career. You are a work in progress.

What is important is that you continue to move forward towards a better position than you were in yesterday.

Why not start a diary listing your accomplishments, milestones and breakthroughs? Then take a minute to reflect on all that you've done.

2. Add some love to your life

"Enjoy the little things, for one day you may look back and realize they were the big things." – Robert Brault

You'll probably have heard the saying "It's the little things that count." These little things are usually the small and often underappreciated aspects of life that make us happy. It could be a cup of coffee, a walk along the beach, going to a yoga class or wearing an outfit that makes you feel special.

Give yourself some time every day to notice – and appreciate – the small things that bring you happiness

3. Do what you love

"Your work is going to fill a large part of your life, and the only way to be truly satisfied is to do what you believe is great work. And the only way to do great work is to love what you do. If you haven't found it yet, keep looking. Don't settle. As with all matters of the heart, you'll know when you find it." – Steve Jobs

By doing what you love for a living, you will have a happier, more productive life, as well as having higher self-esteem and better health.

4. Visualize your perfect day

"To accomplish great things, we must first dream, then visualize, then plan...believe...act!" – Alfred A. Montapert

Every day of your life is down to you. Everyone has the same time to work with. It's up to you to decide how to fill those 24 hours.

Be honest and ask yourself if you're wasting time watching reality TV, not getting up early, being grumpy about your job, or generally wishing for a better, more fulfilling life. Then ask yourself if you're going to chase your dreams and do whatever it takes to reach them.

Three steps to the perfect day:

You have to do the work yourself – and you have the power to do it. No-one else can do it for you.

Write down what your perfect day looks like.

Believe 100% that your perfect day can become reality.

Take 5 minutes in the morning after the first two steps to visualize the day and what you want to happen.

5. Put yourself first

"Love yourself first and everything else falls into line. You really have to love yourself to get anything done in the world." – Lucille Ball

It's OK to be selfish and put yourself first. It's admirable to help others, however don't forget to pay attention to your own needs. Treat yourself to a massage or beauty treatment. Go on a weekend trip and disconnect from an always-connected world.

Block out time that's all for you, and don't share it with anyone else.

6. Tell yourself everything is awesome

"Success is a state of mind. If you want success, start thinking of yourself as a success." – Dr. Joyce Brothers

Happiness. It comes from within and comes from a positive mindset. Believe in yourself, no matter what you face, and your life will be more positive.

7. No-one is perfect

"If you look for perfection, you'll never be content." – Leo Tolstoy

Do you ever look at someone and feel a tinge of jealousy because they're so confident? Well, you shouldn't, because sometimes, deep down, they're insecure too.

The world is imperfect, and you need to stop comparing yourself to others. Your happiness is not worth playing "Keeping up with the Joneses".

When you accept yourself for who you are, your life becomes simpler, more peaceful and more fulfilling.

8. Surround yourself with positive people

"Surround yourself with only people who are going to lift you higher." – Oprah Winfrey

Your friends should bring out the best in you and help you to reach new levels in life. Think about the people you spend your time with in terms of quality instead of quantity.

Your life will be happier with just a few quality friends who inspire you and make you feel like you can do anything, than 30 friends who leave you feeling down and like you're not good enough.

9. Don't waste time worrying

"Stop worrying about what you have to lose and start focusing on what you have to gain." – Author unknown

You can do anything in life. There are endless possibilities and outcomes. Remember, whatever is going to happen will happen, whether you worry about it or not.

Stop wasting time worrying about things you have no control over. If you can't do anything about the problem, then move on and get on with your own life – without the things you can control.

10. Move out of your comfort zone

"Move out of your comfort zone. You can only grow if you are willing to feel awkward and uncomfortable when you try something new." – Brian Tracy

We cannot become what we want to be by remaining what we are." – Max Depree

Nothing worth having comes easy – or with any guarantee of success. Life is all about being willing to take risks.

If you're in your comfort zone, your world becomes much smaller, you lose sight of what's truly important and you'll generally feel unhappy. Instead of thinking "If only I had..." – try taking that leap of faith and perhaps you'll discover the life you've always dreamed of.

11. Get a go-to song

"Words make you think. Music makes you feel. A song makes you feel a thought." — Yip Harburg

Pick a song that makes you feel good, and make that your go-to song when you're having a bad day. Studies show that music can make us feel happier, even on the worst of days.

Chapter 27: The New You

Express gratitude.

Give thanks for every positive thing in your life. It's not always about counting your blessings. It's appreciating them and acknowledging them no matter how small they are. Time, chance, and moment are also to be thanked for. What does this mean? For example, you are up for a spot to go on a big 3-day conference to represent your company. Unfortunately, something came up and the spot was given to someone else. That is a big blow, of course, but you went home and spent the next 3 days with your daughter. Later on, you heard your child say a prayer of thanks for finally giving her a chance to bond with you and heard her whisper how it will be a memory she would forever treasure. You see, here you are given a chance, a time, and a moment. Express gratitude for that.

Simple gratitude can help maintain a positive environment for you and the people around you. Gratitude has a ripple effect. You thank for what you were given and what shall be given to you, and when you are granted either a want or a need, you again say a prayer of thanks. When you live a life, no matter how trivial it is, the positive energy spreads in your life and those lives affected by yours as well as long as you are filled with gratitude.

It boosts the conscious effort of living a positive life. Affirmation is another key to attraction. We create our life through the way we think anyway. Affirm your dreams and your goals. Do not tie the two with negative thoughts. Do not envision a road filled with hindrances and hurdles. Accept that it may, but do not assume that it will.

This may be a cliché but try to live a fruitful life. Do you want to look back and remember having lived your life with only so much negativity? Life does not hold certainty. It is not so much what will happen but what we want to happen and what we will do with what will happen. It is about how we will experience life to the fullest with all that goes with it.

The shift from being a negative thinker to being a positive thinker rests solely in your hands, but remember chapter 4. Visualize a life as a positive thinker. Visualize it until you live it. There are so many opportunities and beautiful moments that await you when you quell your worries and fears.

Chapter 28: How To Adopt This

Attitude Now

"The only thing that's Capital-T True is that you get to decide how you see things."

David Foster Wallace

I know you want to get to the do this and do that part. And we shall be there in a while. You are probably imagining that this is going to be hard. I want to make this as easy for you as possible. First, am going to give you things that have short effect. These you effect now. These will enable you create some momentum and turn your life around. The interesting bit is that much of them have been sprinkled some wherein the book.

Now let's get one thing clear. Our minds have an amazing way of hiding the actual truth. You don't want to think positively. Yes you heard me right. Nor do you even want to control your negative thoughts.

You don't even don't want to get rid of any emotions at all. All you want to do is understand yourself, to enable you arouse the courage to go for the goal you really want to achieve, despite your doubts and your limitations. As such, many of the solutions to positive thinking is not exactly about how to think more positively nor less negatively. Rather, how to deal with yourself on a deep level. How to deal with your insecurities? How to handle not having control over things? This is the how to be confortable of being uncomfortable. Arousing the courageous step-up towards you want in life. Without further ado.

• Accepting yourself

In order for you to focus fully on the results that you want in any area of life. You will have to accept and appreciate your self the way you are. You are a human being, with insecurities, fears, and with self-imposed limitations. Accepting yourself means that what is- Is. What is not is not. Many of the self-doubts and negative thoughts that come to your mind are caused by the feeling and placing yourself in a less privileged position. We compare ourselves with others and this makes us feel like we are less worthy. This causes us to even doubt how much we want what we are striving to achieve. This is a big mind shift to make if you are to make any progress. This is the first step to improving any area of your life. Also accept that where you are is where you are. And that that's where you are going to start from. There are no cheat sheets.

• Take responsibility

Accepting yourself as mentioned above relieve you of many worries. Worries of your ability to fall through. It gives you the power to know that you and only you decide what is important in your life. It's liberating to know that only YOU can take the effort to make anything possible in your world. Taking responsibility makes you your own man on a white horse saving you.

- Don't take things so seriously

I want you to go in front of the mirror now. Make a funny face. This is one sound a bit stupid but trust me do it. Smile. Relax your face.

How does that feel. You have got to let yourself loosen up. Learn to smile every day. Smiling and laughing releases any built up tension within your face and body. Being able to conjure a smile even while striving in different aspects enforces in your mind that it will be fine no matter what.

- Visualization

This serves to give you clarity and direction on what you value. I want you to sit down and open google search engine. Imagine everything you want to own, imagine how you want to look like, and imagine how you want to feel. Type it in the browser search and click on images.

Now get all the images that capture exactly what you want to have, be, feel and achieve in your life. Assemble them into some kind of mosaic. If you can't access google. Use magazine/newspaper picture cutouts and glue on a chart or board. I would further encourage you to go ahead and hang it where you will see it. If you use google images. Creating a collage and placing it as your wall paper will do. Creating a picture of the things you want to achieve helps you focus on your goals and leave no room for negative emotions to conjure up.

Now every day I want you to look at that picture collage. Do it to the point where you feel you deserve every single thing on it. No more excuses here, this isn't hard. Just look at your collage, touch the pictures there and say I deserve all this. Every morning when you wake up and evening before bed.

- Watching your mind

178

When our minds are going AWOL on us. We usually feel it. We feel when our energy is dwindling. We know when we are experiencing doubts. We know when our minds are at cross roads. The best way to watch our mind is to call fact or fiction on the emotions we are experiencing. For instance if you are feeling a sensation of fear. You have to ask yourself are you scared or you are thinking you are scared. Many times, things that are a real scare don't first wait for us to realise and rationalise. When something is a real threat we usually just act. Imagine you are in the middle of the road and a huge truck is coming your way. Do you wait and rationalize whether it will kill you or not? Probably not. You just act by getting out of the way. In the same spirit if you find catch your self realising these different emotions of fears, worry, and doubt or any other for that matter. Just simply understand these are fig mates of your super active imagination. You are probably not scared it's just your mind making such association.

- Affirmations

In this exercise, we want to make our minds doubt proof. We need to affirm that we are good enough to do it. Just taking five minutes in the morning and five minutes before you sleep and meditate upon the things you did right each day will make a significant difference in your life. You will understand that despite yesterday not being a perfect day, there were small wins that you achieved today and that you are still alive.

For affirmation I want you to get up each morning and write down

I am 100% responsible for my success with…. (Put whatever...You want to achieve…) and am also responsible for creating the opportunities leading to that success.

Write that statement everyday morning and evening. After a few weeks you will feel so empowered that you will want to pay me….100 dollars for this tip.

• Keeping a success journal

The fastest way to achieving a goal is to track it. Every single aspect, writing down your successes and failures towards it every day. Writing down the successes and failures creates what we have been calling the positive thinking mindset. It lets you re-live your day without the emotional attachment. It gives you the whole spectrums of life as you lived it but this time outside all the heat. While journaling, it's important to understand that you are focusing on identifying the goals that you planned to achieve that day and if you achieved them or not. In doing this, your mind shows you the other options that you would have taken. So that next time such a scenario comes around, you are better prepared.

Chapter 29: Eliminating Negative Triggers

Much like you need positive triggers to get you started with positive thinking, you also need mechanisms to fight negative thinking triggers.

Here are a few tips for breaking negative thinking triggers.

1. Breaking Old Patterns

To break negative triggers when you are trying to give up a bad habit, start doing something that is drastically different from your regular routine. When you are stuck in the old routine or way of doing things (even if it isn't directly related to the habit you are trying to give up), you are likelier to slip back into the old habit. This leads to more negative thinking.

If you are trying to break a bad habit or negative pattern, try to visualize yourself as a flexible person and do small yet different things. Try to eat something you haven't tried earlier. Visit a new museum in your city. Try taking a completely different route to and from work. Go shopping to a place where you haven't been before. Watch a genre of film you don't normally consider. Breaking a pattern where these small, everyday things are concerned will make it easier for you to stay away from a negative, destructive routine you're following earlier.

2. Visualize Negative Thoughts as Flames

Each time you witness a negative thought trigger, view it as a tiny flame burning in a huge space or an empty lot. It can't cause much harm. Allow the flame to extinguish or burn out on its own. It is powerless and helpless compared to the space where it is kept.

Your mind is like the huge, unoccupied parking lot. One tiny negative trigger or thought doesn't have the power to envelope it. It is insignificant and inconsequential compared to the power of your mind.

3. Move On

If you are filled with regret about a decision you've made in the past, here is a clever and effective hack to eliminate negative triggers of guilt and regret form your mind.

Xiuping Li, a researcher from the National University of Singapore Business School, asked a few participants to pen down a recent decision they had taken that they now regretted. Li then instructed them to seal the envelopes.

Post this exercise, the ones who sealed their envelopes reported to feeling considerably better about past decisions than participants who didn't seal their envelopes. This simple symbolic gesture could bring about a shift in their subconscious mind.

The next time, you find yourself overcome by negative triggers simply write them on a piece of paper and seal it or burn it or throw it away. This way you are signaling to your subconscious mind that you are done with the matter, and it is now time to move on. Kissing your past decisions goodbye by sealing them in an envelope is an effective way of getting over the regret of a lost client or an incorrect business decision. Converting the decision into an ash pile is also a good idea!

When negative thoughts are linked to a very clear and overpowering emotion such as jealousy, anger, and fear, remove all your pent-up negativity by writing it on a piece of paper. Let your thoughts flow in an unedited and uninterrupted manner. Later, destroy this paper as a symbol of your commitment to let go and move on.

If you aren't word savvy, use art to create similar results. For instance, you can mold the negativity trigger in clay or sculpt it or sketch it. Once you give it a form or physical representation, it is easier to destroy it as a symbol of wanting to move on. It is a self-satisfying gesture that allows you to experience an emotional catharsis and dump negative thoughts.

4. Keep Eyes Fixated on the Bigger Picture

One of the best ways to free yourself from the negative thinking pattern is to keep your eyes firmly fixated on the bigger picture.

For instance, if you are working hard towards meeting your goal of taking your family for a vacation, you'll overcome challenges and seemingly negative situations more effectively by keeping your eyes. You won't worry about the fussy client or boss from hell as these small triggers will feel inconsequential if you think about the bigger picture.

Think about a situation when you leave your house for work without any umbrella, and it starts raining. There are two options—you either wince about not having an umbrella and spoil your entire day or keep your eyes fixated on the day's objectives. If you choose to do the latter, you just enjoy the feeling of soaking up the refreshing rain on your skin. When we have our eyes on the larger picture, a few small challenges here and there seem irrelevant. We increase our ability to bounce back from seemingly negative thoughts and situations.

5. Replace Negativity in Surroundings

Your surroundings can have several triggers that can activate a destructive loop of negative thinking. Think about all the things within your immediate surroundings that lead you to a negative thought pattern. It can be anything from a magazine to social media to a song. How much time do you spend on these triggers?

Now, ask yourself what you can do to reduce or eliminate exposure to these negative thinking triggers. For instance, if a bunch of magazines in your house is leading you to have negative self-image issues or think negatively about your appearance, limit exposure to it. Stop buying these magazines or subscribing to them. Instead, read business, hobby-related, or motivational stuff that leads you closer to your goals.

Similarly, if you slip into negative thinking after going through your social media feed, limit the time you spend on Facebook or Instagram. Instead, try to read informative stuff that increases your knowledge and keeps you up-to-date with your industry. Go through inspiring blogs and pages.

6. Keep a Thought Journal

Use a thought journal for identifying negative triggers and where they can impact your overall thinking. Sometimes, we cannot even identify these triggers because they happen to affect us at a subconscious level.

Keeping a journal and noting your thoughts in the journal when negative thoughts arise will help you not just identify these triggers but also determine your action in response to them. Our negative thoughts are so deeply conditioned that they are often involuntary reflex reactions.

Take a few moments to write about how you feel when some trigger doesn't make you feel particularly good. What was it that caused you to think negatively? How did you feel when the negative thought occurred? What was your body's reaction to the negative trigger?

7. Stop the Thought in its Tracks

When you feel a negative trigger slowly consuming your mind with negative thoughts, perform some physical action that will snap you out of the loop. For instance, if you find yourself thinking negatively about something or someone, stop yourself in the track with a discomfort causing physical action such as biting your lips or pinching your hand. This will send a signal to the mind to stop the thought right in its tracks.

Some people simply say "stop" aloud to hold the thought. You can also use more stronger and colorful language to tell the negative thought to "get lost." Another technique that works well is to have a big, bright red stop sign in front of you where you can spot it all the time at a place where you are most likely to come up with negative thoughts.

For example, if you are constantly having negative thoughts on your work desk, keep a red, stop sign handy somewhere where you can spot it immediately when you start thinking about your monster boss or client. It is a visual clue that makes your negative thoughts stop in its tracks.

We know of a person who splashes water on his face each time he thinks he is about to slip into a negative thought pattern. He simply walks into the restroom and keeps splashing water on his face until the thought is forced to fade away. It may seem insane, but it's a brilliant tactic to combat negative thoughts.

8. Enforce Boundaries

If you have been thinking negatively for long now, it is going to be challenging to suddenly start thinking positively. The middle way is to let enforce boundaries or keep a fixed time until which you will allow yourself to think negative thoughts. However, after the set time is over, you cannot think about it any further. Entertain your negative thoughts for a limited and fixed duration rather than letting them linger on forever.

This means you won't indulge them all the time but only during the fixed duration. For instance, just like you have a cheat day for a diet plan, have a negative thinking time window for a few weeks.

Rather than forcing yourself to snap out of negative thinking instantly and start thinking positively (which is tough), get yourself habituated into giving up negative thinking gradually but steadily. Try enforcing boundaries for a few weeks before giving up negative thinking. Sometimes, allowing a negative thought to live its life will stop it from rearing its ugly head every time in the future.

Difference Between Subjective and Objective Thoughts That Impact Our Thinking

We all know the difference between subjective and objective. Objectivity, in a general context, refers to anything that isn't impacted by personal feelings or prejudices. Rather, it is based on unbiased facts. Unlike subjectivity, there is no place for personal interpretations, emotions, views, or feelings.

Subjectivity, on the other hand, is a product of an individual or personal evaluation about something or someone. It doesn't relate to cold, hard facts but feelings and personal interpretations.

When you want to bring about a shift in your thoughts from negative to positive, the perception of the conscious mind needs to be altered. This is easier to accomplish for subjective thoughts because they are based on personal interpretations.

With simple practices such as yoga, meditation, affirmation, journaling, and other techniques, you can reprogram your brain to think in a more balanced or objective manner, thus minimizing the risk of negative thinking.

When you attempt to bring about a change in your perspective, you try to convert a subjective thought into objective so that you can think about it in a more balanced and rational manner.

Let us take an example. You have something exciting to share with your partner,and he/she isn't taking your call. If you think subjectively, you are likely to come up with several reasons why they aren't answering your call. You will start thinking negatively by personalizing the act of not answering your call. Are they having an affair and therefore are out with someone else? Have they stopped caring about you because they found someone better? These are all based on your subjective interpretations of why you think they are not answering your call.

However, now if you decide to change the approach to neutral or positive thinking, you will start looking for facts and more realistic possibilities rather than thinking in extremes. Facts such as these are the time when they have maximum client meetings scheduled, which means they may very well have been caught up in another meeting. You generally do not call them at this time, so they aren't expecting a call from you and have put their phone in a meeting mode.

What you are doing is turning a seemingly subjective thought on its head and lending it greater objectivity to get out of the negative thinking pattern.

When we determine what thoughts have power and don't, there are two distinct types. Objective thoughts are more a result of reasoning, research, analysis, study, recollection of facts, etc. It is a direct result of activities related to your intellect.

Subjective thinking, on the other hand, has undercurrents of feelings, emotions, perceptions, and activities of the "heart."

Therefore, when things go wrong once, base your thinking on facts. What are the chances of it going wrong again? How many times have things actually gone wrong? If you think subjectively, you'll think if it went wrong once, it will go wrong each time. This will lead to negative thinking.

Chapter 30: Putting Positive Thinking Into Practice

It is easy to talk about positive thinking, but it can be quite hard to apply. You can say that you will never harbor negative thoughts again, but when you find yourself in a stressful situation, you may start losing confidence and having negative self-talk. You may also harbor negative thoughts when you experience obstacles, make mistakes, encounter toxic people, or be in unfavorable circumstances.

Then again, if you are truly determined to put positive thinking into practice, all of these negativities will not be able to prevent you from doing so. Positive thinking takes practice. The more you do it, the better you get at it. If you continue practicing it, it will soon become a habit. I can't stress that last point enough. Practice makes positive, and positive makes perfect.

Comparisons Between Negative and Positive Phrases

At times, it becomes confusing to distinguish negative phrases from positive ones. This is especially true if you have been used to speaking negatively. A lot of people are actually inclined to having negative communication.

First of all, you have to be aware of negative self-talk. Keep in mind that the way you speak to yourself sets the tone to how you treat yourself. If you keep telling yourself that you are ugly, dumb, or incapable of doing things, your confidence level will get lower and you will not be able to achieve your goals. When you engage in negative self-talk, you sabotage yourself before you even try doing something.

For example, if you are in a beauty pageant and you see that all the other contestants are beautiful, you must not engage in negative self-talk. If you tell yourself that you are ugly and fat compared to the other ladies in the pageant, you will not feel confident enough to carry yourself. If you tell yourself that you will never win because you do not stand a chance against them, you will not be able to perform your best.

Likewise, if you are at a job interview and you keep telling yourself that you will not get hired, you will not be able to give good answers to the interviewer's questions. If your self-esteem is low, you will also not be able to walk around with confidence or sit down with ease. You will look and act nervous and you will seem incompetent. You see, you have already sabotaged yourself before you even gave yourself a chance to show what you got.

You may also want to rephrase your sentences when you talk to yourself. For example, when you make a mistake, you can tell yourself that it is a good learning experience instead of beating yourself up for it. You can say "I did not win the beauty pageant this year, but this gives me another chance to prepare for next year" instead of "I did not win because I am not as beautiful or as tall as the other candidates." You can also say "This divorce gives me the opportunity to be on my own and do the things that I am passionate about" instead of "This divorce makes me miserable because I have no one and nobody loves me."

Negative phrases are easier to turn into positive phrases when you look at the bright side of things. Even in the most difficult circumstances, positive people are still able to see the light. You just have to examine your situation from different angles. You also have to be rational and not get carried away by your current emotions. When you become logical, you will see that there are ways on how you can make things better.

When it comes to communicating with other people, you also have to be mindful of what you say and how you deliver it.

You have to be extra careful when you are pressured or when your time is limited. Once your words are out, there is no way you can get them back. Therefore, you must not allow your impatience or temper to get the best of you and negatively affect your communication.

While it is true that you do not have control over the way other people perceive phrases and sentences, you can still have a significant contribution to it. For example, negative communication may occur when you ignore the feelings of other people, when you do not express your feelings properly, and when you do not show respect towards others.

On the other hand, positive communication may occur when you express your thoughts and feelings directly, you acknowledge the feelings of others, and you display a caring and respectful attitude towards others.

"I've never done that before < It's an opportunity to learn something new"

There is another difference between positive people and negative people. Positive people have a welcoming attitude towards new ideas while negative people prefer to get stuck in their old ways. Positive people are willing to take risks if it means that they can improve themselves or be in a better position while negative people are afraid to get out of their comfort zones because they think that they cannot bounce back in case failure occurs.

So, if you refuse to try new ideas or do things that you have never done before because you are afraid of failing, then you are a negative person. On the other hand, if you always take every opportunity as something that can lead to growth, prosperity, and success, then you are a positive person. Negative people are cowards but positive people are courageous.

If you keep staying where you are, you will never move forward. You may even be tempted to go backwards because you are too anxious about the future. Your negative thoughts hinder you from taking chances and making mistakes, which are all crucial for growth and success. If you want to be happy and successful, you have to accept the fact that nothing is certain. However, you have a much better chance of improving if you are willing to take risks and have no problem using mistakes and failures as learning experiences.

Practicing Positive Thinking Everyday

Positive thinking can make you healthier, happier, and more productive. It can also help you influence others. To help you practice positive thinking on a daily basis, you must follow these guidelines:

Guide your energy.

What does that mean? It means that you have to have positive thoughts in order to have positive energies. Quantum physics states that the vibrations you send out are what you attract. So, if you have positive energy, positive things will come to you. You will receive more blessings and love into your life. You will be happier and more successful.

Practice visualization.

According to Buddha, you become what you think of. So, if you think of yourself as a happy and successful person, you will really become a happy and successful person. Conversely, if you see yourself as a sad, cynical person, you will really live a miserable life. Your mind is very powerful. You have to use your powers wisely.

In psychology, creative visualization is the practice of aiming to affect the external world through changes in expectations and thoughts. When you practice visualization, you are able to do things that you previously did not think you can accomplish.

Be compassionate.

According to the Dalai Lama, you have to be compassionate if you want other people to be happy. Likewise, you have to be compassionate if you want yourself to be happy.

Yes, it may be hard to remain positive and calm when you are facing so much failures and adversities. However, you must view these things as challenges that you can overcome rather than punishments or situations that you can never get out of.

You have to be compassionate towards yourself and other people so that you can better understand situations. Do not blame yourself and do not blame others. Without compassion, you will not obtain the awareness that will help you nurture yourself.

Be resilient.

Positive people are resilient. Just like everyone else, they also experience loss. They make mistakes, lose loved ones, lose property, fail in business, etc. They are just like you. However, they choose to stay resilient amidst crisis and chaos. They are able to adapt, accept, and practice gratitude.

Chapter 31: Can You "Force" Yourself

Into Happiness?

Here's the scenario:

• Your boss has been bugging you for an entire week to get that presentation done.

• You discover that one of your kids have caused some trouble in school and he was sent to a detention class by the teacher.

• Your washing machine and refrigerator have broken simultaneously and it's going to cost several thousands of dollars to fix.

You can add a few more incidents if you want.

The point is when these are conditions happen, concurrently or separately, they probably aren't going to make you happy. However, a better question is, can you actually make yourself happy just by changing how you think? There's plenty of evidence to support that you can indeed force yourself to be happy. In fact, it's been scientifically proven that by forcing yourself to smile for just 2 minutes, there's a radical shift in your chemistry and psychology, which can be the catalyst for the turnaround.

While it won't make all the day-to-day problems disappear, it will surely help make life easier. One way to reinforce this happiness is to focus your thinking on all the things you have in life, rather than those transient problems. Those problems will eventually go away. You will finish your boss's presentation and he'll leave you for peace (for a minute maybe). You will work with your kid that is having trouble and get him some extra help.

You will find the money required to fix the home appliances and they will run smoothly again. If you can picture those positive outcomes, the actual problems themselves will become less important.

Set up a vision of what it's like to be happy and your brain will work to help you get there. When you are happy, the people whom you work with or live with will naturally pick up your mood and they will be positively affected.

Of course, there are certain times when no matter how hard you try, you simply can't get past feeling a bit de-motivated. In those instances, it's always better to talk to friends and family.

Sometimes, just having someone listening to you can shift your mood around. A few of those people may even give you some constructive advice on how to solve the problems you are facing and this can help you lighten the burden, which eventually set you up for happiness and other positive emotions.

Another way to make yourself happier is to take a break once in a while.

Spend some time in solitude and nature. Read an inspirational book. Go for a mini vacation with your family and kids.

People need to realize the importance of recharging themselves and getting away from the usual routines. It lets you see life from a different perspective and allows you to think more clearly and broadly. This can be all that is needed to break through tough challenges and negative situations so that you are relieved and can go back to experience your default setting of happiness.

Trademarks of Happy Folks

Why are some individuals delighted all the time? The happiest individuals have practices that raise the chances of feeling happy. Unhappy people have practices that lead to less preferable sensations. It can be that basic. If you're not as happy as you'd like, take a look at your habits and practices.

Those that are happy share numerous qualities. Embracing these same qualities will yield positive results.

Practices that lead to joy are enjoyable to carry out:

1. Optimism. Undoubtedly, if you think good things will occur, it's far more likely that you'll be happy. Expecting the worst not does anything to improve your state of mind! Realistically, it's not even crucial to expect a favorable result, only to think that everything will be okay. Optimism is also a form of belief in yourself. If you think that you can deal with any situation,

you can be positive and have the psychological freedom to be happy.

2. Altruism. Doing things for others offers numerous benefits. You can see firsthand that you have a lot to be grateful for. You can feel great about yourself for assisting others. You have a great reason to leave your home. You also feel helpful and useful. Make a list of a minimum of 3 ways you can assist others that will also suit your schedule.

3. Gratitude. Do you recognize how many fantastic things and individuals you already have in your life? By focusing on the things you don't have, you're making yourself dissatisfied and unhappy. Experiencing gratitude assists in developing sensations of joy.

4. An exciting future. Maximum happiness requires that you have something to

eagerly anticipate. It can be finishing college, having a child, retirement, a getaway, or a hot date on Saturday night. Have a couple of goals that give you a reason to be delighted. Have goals and objectives that are both short-term and long-term.

5. Success. Spend some time doing tasks that you're good at. It feels great to do well at something. It does not need to be a competitive event. You can hit baseballs at the batting cage or play the guitar and feel excellent about yourself. Make a list of the things you are really good at and aim to spend at least a little time each day doing them.

6. Durability. It's difficult to prevent challenging times. Sooner or later, something will happen that threatens your development, success, or happiness. Durability is the capability to continue forging ahead. Some people have a flair

for making challenges seem bigger than they truly are. Others are able to maintain their composure and continue making progress.

7. Realistic expectations. When your expectations are overly optimistic, you'll consistently experience disappointment. When your expectations are regularly low, you will not feel very positive. Neither is a recipe for happiness.

8. Forgiveness. How can you be happy while holding a grudge? Forgiving others quickly and easily makes happiness possible. You might feel that some individuals don't deserve forgiveness, but exactly what is the alternative? Making yourself miserable and unhappy.

9. Authenticity. Spending your time pretending to be something you're not is a challenge to your self-esteem. Joy is

allusive if you do not feel comfortable being yourself. Allow your individuality to shine through.

10. Presence. Thinking about the failures of the past can lead to feelings of regret. Thoughts of the unknown future can lead to anxiety. Keep your mind in the present if you want to experience happiness regularly.

There's absolutely nothing complex about happiness. Forgive others, be yourself, offer of yourself, and be grateful for the important things and people you already have. Having a reliable set of habits will lead to feeling more happiness.

Chapter 32: How To Solve Personal Problems

Our weakness is our lack of deep problem-solving techniques. We have the notion that if medicine can't cure it, then, it cannot be fixed. This smart fix mentality has given rise to multi-million drug industries. The problem is that we buy knowing that the problem we are trying to cure can only be solved by looking deeper.

As humans, we have that one underlying issue that tortures us regularly. Often, we hide this issue. These problems could be addictions, anxiety, jealousy, inferiority, overeating and much more.

• The way forward

The real solution starts when you approach the problem. However, many of us expect a magic bullet or instant remedy, and when we do not find it, we give up easily. Also, we don't reveal the truth to those who want to assist us and approach the problem with negativity.

• Give the problem respect

Do not hate the monster, or try to kill it because it has survived long enough despite you trying to eliminate it. The truth is, it may become even stronger as it resists. Take time, and think about it

• The problem is your greatest teacher

The moment you will agree that the inner problem is your teacher; the change will begin. If you only listen, you will realize that you have a lot to learn from your inner problem.

• Avoid looking for a magic bullet

• Investigate underlying attachments

This is the cause. Nobody prefers to encounter a problem, but when you have it, you are the one responsible. Also, know that you will have a hard time identifying it.

• Have someone to talk to

Do not feel ashamed or afraid. Share your problem with someone who has experienced the same. Sharing the problem attracts solutions.

Chapter 33: Ways To Overcome

Negative Thinking For Good

Just as powerful as positive thinking, negative thinking can also be a powerful tool that can devastate an individual's life.

Your thoughts discern how you feel every day, how you perceive the world, and what you think and feel about other people. Your way of thinking discerns most of your behavior.

With positive thinking, you can never go wrong. It is driven by your determination and faith that there is always good in a situation, event, thing, or person. On the other hand, with negative thinking, your life can turn towards the downward slope. As such, it is best to overcome negative thinking for good.

Negative thinking can be brought about through different patterns and ways. It is necessary to first recognize the types of negative thoughts in order to be aware if they are about to occur.

There are four significant ways to overcome negative thinking for good. These include recognizing negative thought patterns, disengaging from negative thinking, being mindful of the moment, and choosing constructive thoughts over destructive ones.

1.   Recognizing negative thought patterns

Negative thought patterns are unproductive thoughts, which are repetitive. They have no real purpose and cause negative emotions. Once you learn to recognize, as well as identity, your thought patterns as they transpire, you can begin choosing your manner of reacting to a situation.

Some of the most common negative thought patterns include: anxious thoughts and worry, regret and guilt, and other problems.

2.   Disengage from negative thinking

If you are a prisoner of negative thinking, chances are you feel hopeless because you do not know what to do. However, it is necessary to face your fears and problems. You need to plan your future. You have to face and deal with every situation that life gives you. Thus, you need to be free from negativity. You should not be identified with negative thinking.

You can start by focusing more of your attention on what goes inside your mind at a given situation. Be a better observer of your surroundings and inner environment. Through having conscious attention of your thinking patterns, you create a new and improved awareness. Thus, you will be able to step back from negative thoughts until such time that they no longer have a hold on you.

3. Being mindful of the moment

Most negative thoughts come from two tendencies of the mind. One is dwelling on the past and the other is worrying about the future. Dwelling on the past involves overly contemplating your problems, mistakes, guilt, or anything unpleasant that may have happened in the past. It involves dwelling over things that should have gone the way you perceived it should have. On the other hand, worrying about the future involves fear of what might and might not happen to you, others, or the world.

In order to step out of your negative thinking process, give the present moment your absolute attention. Redirect your attention out of the past or future into today and now. All you need to do is use your senses optimally, become aware of your present surroundings, and just be aware of what you experience right at this moment.

4.   Choosing constructive thoughts over destructive thoughts

Once you have developed your inner awareness, you can consciously choose to change your thinking to constructive instead of destructive. Constructive or positive thoughts can help you face daily situations efficiently and successfully.

Dwelling on your past would not help you in any way and could only cause unnecessary and negative emotions. However, you can utilize your past experiences in helping you make decisions as well as adapting your actions to every situation.

Worrying can only cause anxiety as well as grief. However, you can buffer it with constructive action, such as fixing a broken wall in your home or taking out travel insurance. When you have done a corresponding constructive action for a specific situation or problem, you can drop all thoughts about it.

Constructive thinking provides you the opportunity to become happy even if things are not doing so well. It helps you deal with problems in an efficient and practical way.

Overcoming negative thinking for good is not an easy task to do. The four ways mentioned above are not "quick fix" methods of discarding negativity instantly. However, the more you practice them, the more you are able to overcome negative thinking.

Practice awareness of your thought patterns as well as what they do to you. The more you practice, the faster you are able to redirect yourself to be mindful of the present.

Overcoming negative thinking can be likened to body building. You try to build muscles and in time, you become mentally and physically strong. You begin to discard old habits of eating unhealthy foods in order to sustain a fit, strong, and healthy body. In the same manner, overcoming negative thinking is trying to engulf your mind with peace and positivity so you will never again be preoccupied with negative thoughts.

Overcoming negative thinking does not mean you will no longer be able to think or feel,, but it is the destructive thoughts that will no longer linger in your mind like they did before.

Chapter 34: Improve Your Self-Talk

By Conquering Your Mind

In this Chapter, we will discuss how to conquer your mind, the first question that comes to mind is, are your mindful or mindfull? Give it a thought for a second before we dive deep by differentiating the two and how it will help you in conquering those thoughts that are flowing in our mind, your mind is like a trickster, can play a lot of tricks on you. We will look at ways to control those thoughts.

Mindfulness of Thoughts

Mindfulness is being conscious of your thinking when you are conscious of your thoughts you can conquer your mind. You are entirely in the present of what is happening, focusing on a single thought can help you control your mind, and you will learn the skills on holding this thought for five minutes. Always be on alert when other feelings are trying to creep in, meditation has been a good practice that will help you focus.

Practicing Meditation

Meditation for ten minutes a day can help you feel more calm and relaxed, and in control of our thoughts most of the times, it leads to a state of calmness of the mind. In this excessive state stress producing activity of the brain is neutralized, this practice will help you focus better, you will be able to concentrate and enhance your performance. Meditation can help reduce depression and anxiety, helps improve concentration and memory.

Breathing Exercise

Breathing exercise will help you decrease stress, anxiety, boost your mood and improve sleep. This exercise is simple if you learn to do it correctly, don't require any unique tool. Belly breathing is effortless and more relaxing.

Choose any position that's is comfortable for you, breath in through your nose, let the breathing come down into your belly, a full deep breath and then breath out. Do this exercise 5 to 10 minutes while relaxing your muscles and if possible closing your eyes, let all the tension and anxiety flow out with the exhaled breath, that way you will feel calmer. This simple exercise will help relax your mind when the mind is right your self-talk will be more positive, focus more on the present the past is past, and there is nothing you can do about it.

Mind Full Thoughts

We are living in the era of social media; people are creating more stress, anxiety and negative comparison that is affecting them. Social networking can be used in a positive way when you are engaging in groups that empower you positively rather than using it to bombard your mind with negative information. For someone who is already depressed, you are causing more mental harm to yourself thereby increasing your negative self-talk by filling your mind with lots of garbage you see on social media. Spend more time on things that will have a positive impact on your life.

People only post their good memories on social media; everybody has their sufferings too. Comparing your life with other is detrimental to your mental health especially if you are prone to anxiety, it will affect how you view yourself. Don't let that shiny lifestyle you see distract you. Focus your energy and time on building up yourself and accomplishing your goals this way you will appreciate yourself and avoid negative self-talk that will trigger due to unnecessary issues.

When your mind wanders in all the things, you become absent in the present moment, invest time in yourself it is where you will live in this lifetime, those things that are not helping you in personal development discard them. Keep a healthy relationship, especially with your spouse if you are married and positive friends. Your mind is your spiritual estate it is your duty to protect it from harmful thoughts from sinking in. Engage yourself in something new, like learning a new language, enroll in music class, attend seminars and learn new skills that will have a positive impact on your life.

Chapter 35: The Self-Assured Mindset

We must trust in ourselves that we have absolute capability to survive, thrive and live a life of greatness. We hold that power within us as explained within the chapters of this book. Trust yourself because you know more than you think. Your mind is an endless source of solutions. Don't make it an endless source of problems. As we explained in the last chapter, it can be if you make that choice.

Trust in yourself, life, the universe, and in your God. A child wakes up in the morning with trust in his heart. That's why children can experience such joy in simple things. Learn to allow the inner child to surface sometimes, because the joys that lie within this area of your mind are endless.

We must believe that we can accomplish every desire we wish. We must believe that we can handle any challenge that we may face. No matter what we go through we must trust that we will be okay and we have the power within us to pick ourselves back up and keep moving forward.

Even when bad things happen and your response is fearful, if you have a self-assured mindset, this will give you the strength to move forward, rather than dwell on problems.

Overall Lesson: You must be sure of yourself. Those who have low self-esteem struggle with doubt, fear and worry because they are unsure of themselves, they don't have any trust in life! Trust who you are. It doesn't matter if you measure up to public approval. What matters is that you approve of who you are. That's the way that you find acceptance of self and this acceptance of self with allow you to be anything that you wish to be. Trust your own intuitive feelings, allow your mind to grow in good health, wealth, success and happiness by feeding it all of the healthy input you can.

Chapter 36: Applying Positive Thinking To Larger Life Goals

Now that you've begun to change the way you think and feel about yourself personally, you can start to apply these new principals to your business life, and love life. The most important thing to remember in all of this is that you must put yourself out there to succeed.

The great men of history never got anything extraordinary accomplished by letting self-doubt creep into their thought process. They were simply driven, and we should be too. It doesn't matter whether we are looking to change the world, or simply live a good honest life, the right attitude can take us there.

"You can have anything you want if you are willing to give up the belief that you can't have it."

– Robert Anthony

Whatever your goal is professionally it is attainable with the right level of commitment. Success is something that sometimes feels so far away when you are just starting out, or you have been the low man on the totem pole at a company for so long.

Moving up in the world is not only possible, but something one should always strive for to get the better life they deserve. In order to get things like promotions, or jobs in a new field you must believe that you are qualified for the job and can do the work.

Let's say you are looking to get promoted in a company, the positive thinking way to help make this a reality would first start with just making sure you have a good attitude. Employers are more apt to trust and promote individuals who have a positive outlook on life.

Negativity is almost never good for business. Using positive thinking in your everyday approach to the tasks allotted to you will help you get more done, and show customers/clients that you're someone they can trust to do the job well. Even if you are the type of person who second guesses yourself, there are ways to change yourself into a positive thinker in the workplace.

Exercise:

The first step to changing yourself into a positive thinker is to let go of your old ways. In the past, maybe you gave up quickly because something seemed too hard.

Perhaps you didn't feel you had the ability to complete tasks that were put before you. What you believe in your head, you make reality in your life. Let's take this famous quote by Winston Churchill and examine it:

"The pessimist sees the difficulty in every opportunity; an optimist sees the opportunity in every difficulty."

- Winston Churchill

This is a perfect example of how your own mental perceptions can totally flip a situation. When you are in a negative "I can't do it" zone, you will look for excuses and ways out.

Many times you will point to just how difficult something is as a reason for not trying or seeing something through to the end. If you can change your method of thinking, difficult situations turn into challenges that present great opportunities.

Chapter 37: Training The Mind To Have Positive Thoughts Always

When you train the mind to think positively, this shall boost self-esteem and make you have control of your life. When you know how the mind works as well as how to continuously have positive thoughts, this can develop many areas of your life such as family, work and social relations. You need to put hard work and effort when you use positive thinking to improve your life so as to fight and alter your present lifestyle and attitude.

Determine the inner negative thought patterns used by your mind. These patterns are:

Catastrophizing: The act of predicting the worst and exaggerating negative events.

Filtering: The act of concentrating solely on the negative.

Personalizing: The act of blaming one's self.

Talk to yourself in a positive way. Take one negative incident that happened to you in the last seven days. Instead of having negative thoughts about that incident, think about it positively. Tell yourself that being scolded by your boss due to your inability to meet a deadline will make you more vigilant about punctuality. Do such positive self-talk whenever you are in a negative situation so that you will train your mind to have a positive thinking pattern.

Throughout your day, utter positive affirmations not for the purpose of lying but for encouraging yourself. One example is, "I will lose weight because I will eat right and exercise regularly." Do not continuously say things which are entirely impossible and untrue such as having the body of a supermodel when in fact you weigh 200 pounds. You will eventually be disillusioned which will strengthen negative thinking. Being positive does not mean being unrealistic.

Check your thoughts in the coming weeks and months that follow. Stop occasionally throughout your day to assess your inner thoughts to verify if they are more positive or negative. Assess your negative thoughts, take the negativity out of them and turn them into positive thoughts.

Have a journal where you can write down all your positive thoughts. Before going to bed in the evening, write down the positive things that happened in your day. When you acknowledge and jot down these good and positive experiences, this shall harness your thought patterns and habits and will train you to think positively.

In the same journal, write down your short-term goals. You do not have to accomplish all of them but just jot down those that you have. Be thankful for them and the ones that you did not fulfill. If you have goals, this gives you hope as well as purpose in your life. It is these two things which will make you live joyfully and positively.

Look for proper ways to manage stressful situations, events and people. You can exercise regularly because this stimulates your brain chemicals such as endorphins to boost your energy levels and improve your mood. Endorphins are the hormones which relieve pain from the body and allow you to relax. A study in the "Psychosomatic Medicine" journal in 2000 says working out half an hour thrice weekly is as useful as consuming prescription medicine for depression.

You can also meditate everyday as this will clear your mind of negative thoughts and make it relax. When you meditate, this refreshes your body and mind.

Be with positive people composed of relatives and friends. If you are with negative people, they will not support your decisions and thoughts and will only make you have negative thoughts. Make new friends who are optimistic and spend time with people who are supportive so that you will have mental clarity should a problematic situation arrive.Psychology Today says if you have people who encourage and uplift you often, they will serve as your shock absorbers from the harmful effects of setbacks and frustrations.

Chapter 38: The Word And Thought Game

"In order to carry a positive action, we must develop here a positive vision! – The Dalai Lama

All the descriptions in the world are simply words. For this exercise, I want you to go through your day and every time you feel a negative thought coming on, counter it with a positive one. If you feel depressed, ask yourself what's the opposite of depression and make an effort to feel that opposite feeling. If you feel cold, think of the sunshine and feel warmth. If you feel anger – think of the words that have been spoken from another person's perspective and feel compassion instead.

Every word that you use in your life has an opposite. If you are always using negative descriptors, the chances are that you feel negative about life. Play a game with the words and replace everything negative in your day today with something positive. If you find yourself grimacing, look in the mirror and smile. If you find yourself being argumentative, try being agreeable. What you are doing is teaching yourself the difference between negative feelings and positive feelings.

Sure, it's a game, but all the negativity that surrounds your life comes from inside your head, so why not change it?

Once you are able to embrace the positive side of life, you will find that life becomes much lighter and happier. Try it with people too. Instead of greeting the world with negativity, wake up in the morning with a smile and continue that smile for the rest of your day. What you will find is that people respond in a very positive way to smiling. Not everyone does, of course, but when you smile, you open up a whole new way of thinking and you are able to see the world from another angle.

The power of your thoughts

If you ever feel negative, you have to accept that the reason for your negativity is because your thoughts are negative. Thus, if you can do something to change that, you can easily get out of a negative state and work toward your dreams in life. It all starts with words and thoughts and you need to work on your thoughts so that they don't start the never-ending cycle of negativity.

In this instance, I would suggest that you think of something that makes you smile. It may be an amusing YouTube video. It may be something that a child said or even a song that makes you smile, but if you can replace negativity with something that makes you smile, you are half way there.

There's a particularly good YouTube video under the title of Pie Face. It's about a Scottish man and his son playing a game together and if you watch this when you feel negative thoughts coming on, you won't be able to help yourself. You will laugh with your whole heart and sometimes that's all you need to lighten up your thoughts. I watch it sometimes when I need a good belly laugh and the amount of stress relief you get from a great belly laugh is amazing. It puts you in a good mood for the rest of the day.

As you work toward your dreams, there are always going to be negative experiences that come along through the process of words or thoughts. They may be your thoughts or words, but if you have taken my advice and learned to meditate on a daily basis, you are less likely to make those kinds of negative mistakes because you think before you speak and you don't attach any judgment to things that people say, so you are making yourself immune to the potential hurt that it can do to you. However, there's another trick you can use to deafen out words that you don't want in your head.

Think of a happy song. Mine is "I'm busy doing nothing," What happens when you get a negative thought process starting in your head is to sing the song to hush the thought and sing it again if you have to. While you are singing silently in your head, you are not really able to hear all those thoughts and it eventually silences them. You are in fact replacing negative thoughts with positive actions. Try to work out what simple tune you can use to drown out your demons. It may seem like a very simple idea but sometimes the simple ideas are the most effective.

The catchword for the day is positivity. That applies to words. It applies to actions and when you use positive words and thoughts as reinforcement of that happy state of affairs, it stays happy and does not go down the road of self-pity.

Chapter 39: They Are All Mine, And Hence I Cannot Let Go

(Inability to let go things)

Letting go helps us to live in a more peaceful state of mind and helps restore our balance. It allows others to be responsible for themselves and for us to take our hands off situations that do not belong to us. This frees us from unnecessary stress.

- Melody Beattie

I understand that one of the major challenge that we human beings face is "letting go". This habit ties us to our past, and does not allow us to concentrate in our present. Psychology says that people with more ego do not have the capability of letting go things. They hold on to grudges, do not forgive easily, and are usually negative by nature.

Letting go is not just restricted to a person, argument, or way of life, it can me anything under the sun that people hold on to. If we hold on to things, it is bound to bring in pain and agony. Over the years, even I have learn to let go of a number of dreams, relationships, goals, etc. Out of my personal experience, what I can say is; letting go of some things especially if it's related to your emotions is just not an easy task. For example; letting go of your bike, which is very old and is not serving good is far easier that letting go of a person whom you dearly loved.Keep in mind that letting go of certain things will take time. For example – parents death, loss of your childhood friend, etc. No one expects that we let go of people, and relationships easily.

Now the question is – "What should we let go, and what should we hold on to"? You may not find an answer to this in any coaching classes, books, counseling, or seminars. These facilitate will certainly bring about a change in your thinking process, but at the end it's you who have to decide. If you identify what holds you back, then work towards it, you will certainly feel a sense of positivity in you. Your perspective towards life will change, and you will become a happier person.

When you have made up your mind to let go, then you have the following choices –

- You genuinely let go

- You just pretend to let go, but somewhere in your mind you are just thinking of that person, relation, or thing.

The reluctance or unwillingness to 'let go' will lead you to a life which is stressful, full of pain, fear, and negativity. The price that you will pay for just one thing will be too high. I understand that it's not an easy task, but once you learn to master it, you will be able to lead a more accomplished life.

The following are a few important to be noted:

1) The biggest, and the most expensive price you pay is lack of inner peace and happiness.

2) When you do not let go of a few believes, behaviors, and relationships, you end up being frustrated and disappointed. All this results in too much negativity in you.

3) Sometimes, people also surrender themselves to the wills and desires of others. In satisfying someone else, they never achieve emotional calmness. This also results in lack of positivity in a person.

4) Life is about living today, but a few of us either bother about past or future. This makes them restless and negative. They will just not find anything good in their present; and hence will not find anything positive, as well.

5) Letting go is considered as one of the best medicine for mental health.

6) Holding on to things will result in negativity, grief, pain, stress, and anger.

7) Letting go is not easy, but mark my words it's worth the effort and time.

8) It's you who has to decide how you take things. If you hold on to them and do not let go, then it will always bother you, and will curb your power to think on positive lines.

9) Understand the fact that you can never let go if you rely on medicines, therapies, stimulants, etc. This is a disease, which will go only if you want, and work towards the same. The rest are only aids!! In this case, you will have to be your own doctor.

10) If you want to live life thoroughly, then live it inside-out, instead of outside-in.

11) If you are not able to let go, then it shows that you are emotionally week.

12) Life will not guarantee you a better tomorrow, but you can work towards the same to make it better.

13) You will not be able to keep others happy, if you yourself are not happy.

ι things, feel inner peace, and
ι... for life is too short to hold on
grudges, fights, and wrong
onships.

free, feel happy!!

etting go means to come to the
realization that some people are a part of
your history, but not a part of your
destiny."

-      Steve Maraboli